Riddles

And

Brain Teasers

The Ultimate Package Of Never Ending Fun, Laughter & Challenge For Kids And Entire Family.

-Mike C. Biehl

Table of Contents I

Table Of Contents II

Brain Teasers

The Best
199+ Unique Brain Teasers
For
All Ages

- Mike C. Biehl

Introduction

Congratulations on purchasing paperback version of *The Best Brain Teasers: 199+ Unique Brain Teasers for All Ages* and thank you for doing so.

Everyone loves a good riddle. Apart from the enjoyment of the challenge, riddles, puzzles, word problems, and even ciphers are an excellent and fun way to keep our brains sharp. As we get older, our brains work harder to the endless amount of information flooding them. Just as it is important to exercise and keep our bodies physically healthy, the same can be said for our brains. Our brains can't lift weights or run marathons, but thankfully, there is a multitude of ways to ensure they continue to perform at their best.

Research has found that individuals with proficient, able brains tend to be healthier and happier in general. Brain teasers have been found to improve memory and boost overall brain function and processing. Frequent mental exercises can prevent mental boredom and can even reduce the risk of cognitive deterioration such as you would find in an individual suffering from dementia.

The value of this to the adult mind alone is great, but brain teasers also serve as a fun way to teach our children good logic and critical thinking.

The following chapters will explore the wide variety of brain teasers available for all ages, and they are sure to both challenge and stretch the mind, giving it the daily "exercise" it needs.

There are plenty of books on this subject on the market, so thanks again for choosing this one! Every effort was made to ensure it is full of as much useful information as possible.

Please enjoy!

Chapter 1: Beginner Level

Riddles can range from easy to near impossible to solve, making them very versatile brain teasers for all ages. Here are some simpler riddles that will be more child appropriate.

1) When I'm young I'm tall but I shrink as I get older. What am I?

2) A pink person lived in a one-story pink house. Everything in the house was pink: pink doors, pink walls, pink curtains, pink refrigerator, even a pink cat! What color were the stairs?

3) What has hands but no fingers?

4) The more I dry, the wetter I get. What am I?

5) Out of the 12 months in a year, how many of them have 28 days?

6) A man went outside for a walk when it started raining and he had no hat or umbrella. His clothes got soaked, his shoes got soaked. Everything was soaked, except for his hair. Not one hair on his head got wet. How is this possible?

7) There once was a cowboy who rode into town on Friday. He stayed in town for three days then left on Friday. How did he do that?

8) A young boy was injured and rushed to the hospital. The emergency room surgeon came in and said, "I can't operate on this boy; he's my son." But the surgeon was not the boy's father. How is that possible?

9) There are three apples sitting in a bowl on the table and you take away two. How many apples do you have?

10) Dana's mom has 3 daughters: One is named Kelly and one is named Betsy. What's the name of the third daughter?

11) Ken threw a ball as hard as he could. It came back to him even though it didn't touch or bounce off of anything. How?

12) I am almost always answered even though I never ask questions. What am I?

13) What has an eye but cannot see?

14) There is one word in the dictionary that is always spelled wrong. Which word is it?

15) I have a neck but no head! What am I?

16) What do rich people need that poor people have and if you eat it, you will die?

17) What is full of keys but can't open any doors?

18) I have four fingers and a thumb, but I am not alive. What am I?

19) What do you find once in a minute, two times in a moment, but never in a thousand years?

20) We come out at night without being called and we vanish in the day but we are not stolen. What are we?

Riddles can be silly and fun, but there are also some that take all the brainpower we can muster to solve. Here are some more challenging riddles that adults will enjoy. Hints are included for some of the longer riddles. Try not to use them!

21) What has space but no room, keys but no locks, and you can enter but can't go outside?

22) The light gives me life, but if it shines directly on me, I die. What am I?

23) I look flat, but I am deep. I have taken lives but I also offer food. I can be beautiful at times, terrifying at others. I can be angry and calm, smooth and turbulent. I have no heart but I can give pleasure along with death. I belong to no one yet I surround what all men desire. What am I?

24) This five-letter word sounds the same when you remove the first letter and it sounds the same when you take away the third letter. It sounds the same if you remove the last letter and it even sounds the same when you take away all three. What word is it?

25) There once was a man who lived on the 35th floor of an apartment building. Every morning he woke up, got dressed, and took the elevator all the way down to the first floor to carry on with his day. When he came home, however, he only rode the elevator to the 20th floor then took the stairs the rest of the way to his apartment. Why would he do that?

26) Fire cannot burn me, water cannot drown me. What am I?

27) What has mountains but not trees, water but no fish, and cities but no houses or buildings?

28) What is in the middle of April and March that cannot be seen at the end of either of those months?

29) There is a boat filled with people out on the water. It's not sinking but when you take a closer look there isn't one single person onboard. How can that be?

30) What one word in the English language has 3 sets of double letters back to back?

31) What one thing always breaks every time you speak?

32) A boy is physically standing behind his father. But his father is also standing behind him. How is that possible?

33) There was a street magician entertaining a crowd one evening. He calls on a boy to help with his next trick and says, "I am going to touch you on the forehead then write your actual name on this piece of white paper. If I lose you can have whatever piece of my magic equipment you want. If I win, you have to pay me $10." The boy smirked, thinking there was no way he could lose. Even if the magician managed to get his name right, he would lie about it and no one would be the wiser. He read the piece of paper in triumph only to realize he had already lost. Why is that?

34) What dress can you never wear?

35) Amy's daughter is my daughter's mother. Who am I to Amy?

36) Two camels stood in the desert facing opposite directions. One facing East, the other facing West. Since they're in the desert, there is no water to cast a reflection but somehow they can see each other without turning around or even moving their heads. How is that possible?

37) A man is building a house out of bricks. How many did he use to complete the project?

38) What can travel around the world while staying confined in a corner?

39) Once you have it, you want to share it, but if you share it, you no longer have it. What is it?

40) You see me every time you look in the water but I never get wet. What am I?

Chapter 2: Pro Level

Logic and math are where things can get a bit more complicated. Who doesn't love math, right? And you can't live without logic. Well, I guess technically you can, but it might become a bit chaotic. These particular puzzles are a bit more on the challenging side. Helpful hints are included for some of them—others you will just have to work out the math. So keep a level head and try not to overthink them.

1) You're stuck in a labyrinth and you have to escape. You run into a room where there are three doors and you must choose one to get out. The first door to the left leads to a rushing river of lava, the door in the middle leads to a deadly Ninja assassin, and the final door on the right leads to a tiger that hasn't eaten in three months. Which door will you choose?

2) An old man dies, leaving behind his two sons. Before he died, he left a will. In his will, he instructed his sons to have a match race on their horses. The son with the slowest horse would win the inheritance. The sons tried to race but soon realized they were both holding their horses back, which would never do. They went to an old wise man to seek advice. After hearing what he had to say, the boys raced again, this time both riding at top speed. What did the wise man say to change their minds?

3) You have an egg you need to boil in exactly 15 minutes, but all you have to measure the time is a 7-minute hourglass and an 11-minute hourglass. How do you do it?

4) A traveler is making his way down a road when he runs into a fork in the path. The left side leads to eternal happiness while the right leads to certain and excruciating death and he has no way of knowing which is which.
There are two brothers at the fork who know the way. One will tell the truth while the other one only tells lies. The man can ask only one question to point him down the right path. What is the question?

5) Four people come to a river with a narrow bridge over it. The bridge can only hold two people at a time. It's also night and they only have one torch between them that they must use when crossing. Person 1 can cross in one minute, person 2 can cross in two minutes, person 3 can cross in five minutes, and person 4 in eight minutes.

Can they all get across in exactly 15 minutes?

6) A census officer went to a man's house to get his information. The man told her he had 3 children. When she asked him how old his children were, he cryptically answered, "the product of their ages is 72 and the sum of their ages is the same as my house number."

The census officer looked at the paperwork to see the house number and then complained at the man that she still did know their ages. To this, he answered, "Oh, I forgot to tell you. My oldest child likes chocolate pudding."

The census officer wrote down their ages and went on her way. How old are the children?

7) Using only addition, how do you add all "8's" together to get to 1,000?

8) Two sons and two fathers sit down at the table to eat breakfast. Each person eats an egg and three eggs get eaten. Explain how.

9) A woman is sitting alone in her hotel room. There is a knock on her door and when she answers it, there is a man standing there. "Oh, I'm sorry," he says. "I thought this was my room." He then walks back down the hall and gets into the elevator. The woman shuts her door, locks it securely, and then immediately calls security. What made her so suspicious?

10) George went across a bridge and met a man carrying a load of wood that was neither straight nor crooked. How can that be?

11) A merchant needs to ship some products. He can put either 8 large or 10 small boxes into one carton to send. He sent 96 total boxes in one shipment. If there were more large boxes that small ones, how many cartons did he send?

12) There is an athlete who can jump for a very long time. However, with every jump, he gets a little more tired. Each jump is half as far as the first one. On his first jump, he makes it half a foot. His second jump is ¼ of a foot, and so on. So at that rate, how many jumps does it take him to travel forward one foot?

13) My sister's name is Mary. She has 2 kids. My name is Elise, I had two kids. Our brother, George has 2 kids and our cousin Sherrie has 2 kids. All in all, how many kids are there?

14) There once was a king who had a beautiful daughter. It was time for her to marry and there were 3 eligible, very intelligent princes in the kingdom. They were all smart, but it was only the best for the princess and he wanted her to marry the smartest of all. The king calls for his wisest advisor to create a grueling

test of intelligence. The winner of the test would marry the princess; the losers would be put to death!

The 3 princes are taken to a room, seated facing each other, and are shown 5 hats: 2 black ones and 3 white ones. They are then blindfolded and each prince gets a hat placed on his head with the remaining hats hidden in another room. The blindfolds are taken off and it is now time for them to guess which color hat is on their own head.

So, pretend you are one of the princes. You see that your opponents each have a white hat on their heads. After a little while, it becomes obvious that the other princes are either unable to figure out their hats' colors or are unwilling to guess because they are unsure. How do you correctly guess which color your hat is?

15) Three great philosophers settle under the shade of a tree and have a lengthy discussion about why things exist in the world. They then drift off to sleep. There are 3 crows in the trees above them; one above each man. They finish digesting their breakfast and leave a "souvenir" on the forehead of each man. The crows then fly away. The philosophers wake up, look at each other, then all start laughing hysterically at the same time...until one of them suddenly stops. Why does he stop laughing?

16) You sit down at a table with twenty coins. 10 of them are currently heads up, 10 are tails up. Wearing a blindfold and

gloves on your hands, how do you get them into two groups with the same number of heads and tails in each group?

17) Emma and Jake live in separate parts of town but go to the same school. Emma leaves 10 minutes earlier for school and meets Jake in the park. Which one is the closest to school when they meet?

18) Three people check out a hotel room for one night for $30. They each pay $10 and go to their room but the owner suddenly realizes he should have only charged them $25 dollars and sends the bellhop up with their $5 change. Each person takes $1 and they give back to the bellhop the remaining $2 since it would be too hard to split it. They then realize they've only spent $9 (making $27) and the bellhop has $2 which only makes $29. What happened to the missing dollar?

19) There are 2 glasses the same size on the table. One has 100ml of lemonade and the other has 100ml of ink. You take one spoonful of lemonade and stir it into the ink, then take a spoonful of the ink/lemonade mixture and stir it back into the lemonade. Which glass now has the least amount of content inside it?

20) And last but not least, here is one of the hardest logic puzzles in the world! The "Blue Eyes" puzzle (Advanced Logic):

There is a group of people on an island all with assorted eye colors and every person is a brilliant logician. In other words, if there is a conclusion to a problem that can be logically deduced, any one of the inhabitants of that island could do it in a heartbeat. However, none of the logicians actually knows the color of their own eyes. Every midnight, a ferry boat arrives at the island. Any of the islanders who have correctly deduced the color of his or her own eyes can leave the island while the others remain. The islanders can all see the eye color of everyone else at all times and they keep track of the number of people with each eye color (not counting themselves, of course) but they *cannot* communicate any other way with each other. And they all know the rules.

So, on this particular island, there are 100 people with blue eyes, 100 brown-eyed people, and one person (the Guru) with green eyes. So any blue-eyed person can see all 100 brown-eyed people, the 99 remaining blue-eyed people, and the green-eyed Guru. But that does not necessarily reveal what color his own eyes are. For all he knows, he could be the 101st brown-eyed person rather than the 100th blue-eyed person. Or his eyes could be a different color entirely.

The Guru can only speak once at a specific time one day in all of their countless years on the island. That day comes and she stands before them all and says, "I can see someone with blue eyes."

Who leaves the island and on which night?

Even kids who don't like math will have fun working out their brains with these math riddles. There are hints for a few of them, but a lot of them just require doing the math the fun way!

21) You buy a cell phone and a case for it that cost a total of $110. The cell phone costs $100 more than the case. How much did the cell phone cost?

22) You give $36 to a spider, $9 to a duck, and $27 to a bumblebee. Based on those numbers, how much money does the cat get?

23) A farmer bought a rooster for laying eggs. If he expects to get 4 eggs a day out of it how many eggs will he have after three weeks?

24) A zookeeper has 100 pairs of animals in his zoo. Two pairs of babies are born to each one of the original animals but unfortunately, 23 animals don't survive. How many animals are left in the zoo?

25) Jack goes to the store and buys 12 apples. On the way home, all *but* 9 get smashed and ruined. How many are left in good condition?

26) It took 6 people 9 hours to build a barn. How many hours would it take 15 people to build that same barn?

27) If eggs are $0.12 a dozen, how many eggs can you buy with a dollar?

28) Cory has $28.75 in his pocket. He buys 3 chocolate chip cookies for $1.50 each, 5 newspapers for $0.50 each, and 5 roses for $1.25 each. He then purchases a pair of sunglasses with the rest of his money. How much did the glasses cost?

29) Mary went to the store to buy a loaf of bread. In her purse, she had 2 quarters, 3 nickels, 4 dimes, and 2 pennies. The loaf cost $0.82 and she had promised to be sure she had exactly one coin left after buying the bread. Which coin did she have remaining?

30) In a strange, alien land, half of 10 is 6, rather than 5. Using the same alien rules what is 1/6th of 30?

Note: some of these are a little tricky!

31) If you multiply this number by any other number the answer is always the same. What is that number?

32) If 2 is company and 3 is a crowd, what is 4 and 5?

33) Katie adds 5 to 9 and gets 2. How did she do that?

34) What weighs more: a ton of bricks or a ton of feathers?

35) I am an odd number. Take away one letter of my name and I become even. What number am I?

36) How many eggs can you put in an empty basket that is 12 inches wide?

37) How many nines are between the numbers 1 and 100?

38) Which is more valuable? One pound of gold coins costing $20 or a half-pound of gold coins costing $40?

39) Why is the longest nose recorded in history only 11 inches long?

40) Jeff has two coins totaling $0.55 (US). One of them is *not* a nickel. What are the two coins?

Chapter 3: Expert Level

Lateral Thinking Puzzles

These types of riddles tend to more of an advanced level and may not be appropriate for children under 13 or 14 years of age. There is usually more than one way to solve a puzzle. Human nature tends to take the linear approach because that's usually the one that makes the most sense. Lateral thinking involves looking at a problem from a different or unexpected point of view. Keep in mind that there is not necessarily only *one* solution to lateral thinking puzzles, but there is a *best* solution. It requires a variety of brainy skills including creativity and an ability to think outside the box to come up with the one with the highest level of satisfaction.

1) There is a barrel of cider sitting on the ground with no lid. One guy looks inside and says, "It's more than half-full." His friend examines the barrel and disagrees. "No, it's less than half-full." How can they easily figure out which one of them is right without using anything to actually measure the cider in the barrel?

2) The 17th and 15th presidents of some foreign country had the same father and mother but they were not brothers or sisters. How is this possible?

3) There are 3 light switches outside of a windowless room. They are connected to 3 light bulb fixtures inside the room. How do you figure out which switch corresponds to which bulb if you can only enter the room one time?

4) You are lost in the woods and come upon a cabin. Inside the cabin, there is an oil lamp, a stove, and a candle. You only have one match so what will you light first?

5) A man hanged himself in a large wooden barn. The barn is completely empty except for the poor man hanging from the middle of the rafter in the center of the barn. The rope around his neck is 10 feet and his feet are about 3 feet off the ground. The nearest wall of the barn is 20 feet away from him and there is no way he could have climbed the walls or the rafters. But he still managed to hang himself. How?

6) There is a carrot, a scarf, and five pieces of coal lying on the grass. No one put them there, but the reason they are there is actually perfectly logical. What is the reason?

7) Vickie had two sons. They were born on the same day of the same month, in the same year and on the same hour but they were not twins. How is this possible?

8) A man receives a box in the mail. Once he opens it he finds a human arm wrapped up inside. He looks at it carefully then sends it to another man. That man also looks at it closely then goes into the woods and buries it. Why?

9) One day, a man died. He made it to Heaven and as he looked around the thousands of people he saw there, he noticed they all looked like they had when they were in their 20's and that they were all naked. He then notices a couple and immediately recognizes them as Adam and Eve. How does he know that?

10) Mindy was driving down the road in a terrible storm when she arrived at a bus stop. There were 3 people waiting there for the bus: an elderly woman who looked like she could die any minute, an old friend who had once saved her from bankruptcy, and a man—literally the man she had been searching for her whole life. She can only take one passenger in her car. So who does she choose?

11) There is a murderer on the loose and one night the police get an anonymous tip with the address of the house the

murderer is inside. They have no idea what this guy looks like—just that his name is Mike. They act on the tip they were given and burst into the house the caller told them to go to. There they found an electrician, a truck driver, a fireman, and an auto mechanic sitting at a table playing poker. The police don't say a word and they immediately arrest the fireman. How did they know it was him?

12) There are 6 eggs on a plate. 6 people each grab an egg but there is still an egg on the plate? How is that?

13) There is a town that is painted all black. A black man in a black outfit and wearing a black mask is in the middle of the street. There is no moon and the street lights don't work. There is a black car without its lights on headed straight towards him but it swerves just in time. How did the driver see him?

14) Mandy says to Candy, "If you sit in this chair, I will bet you $5 that I can get you to get out of it before I finish running around your chair 3 times." Candy says, "No way! You'll cheat and poke me with something to make me move."

Mandy swears she will not touch Candy and if she gets out of the chair, it will be by her own choice. Finally, Candy agrees to the wager but to her chagrin, Mandy does indeed win the $5. How does she win?

15) Farmer Rob has a very beautiful pear tree. He supplies fruit to the local grocer and the grocer wants to know how many pears he can expect to be able to purchase. Farmer Rob knows the tree has 20 branches. Every branch has exactly 10 boughs and every bough grows 5 twigs, and each twig bears one piece of fruit on it. So how many plums will he be able to deliver to the grocer?

16) Dale is 6 feet tall. He holds a glass cup over his head, drops it on the floor, and doesn't spill one drop of water. How is that possible?

17) One day a young man cruises up to the border of his country and then next on a motorcycle. The customs officer see the three big sacks he has on his bike and demands to know what is inside them.

"It's only sand," the man says.

"Oh, sure, like I believe that," says the officer. He makes the man get off the bike and empties out each bag. Sure enough, there is nothing but sand in them. The officer can't believe it. He makes the man wait while he has the sand analyzed, but finally after all the tests come back negative, he gives up. He gathers the sand into new bags for the man, puts them on his motorcycle and sends him on his way.

Two weeks later, the man comes by again riding a motorcycle with bags of sand. The customs officer does the same tests and even some new ones but once again, all he finds is sand. This whole scenario ends up happening every week for almost three years! Then, one week, the man on the bike never shows up. He has seemingly vanished. But after a short amount of time, who else would the customs officer run across in a restaurant but the sand guy!

The officer marches up to him and says, "Okay, this has been driving me crazy! I know you have been smuggling something all this time, I just don't know what! I'm off duty and I'm not interested in making an arrest. I just have to know: what have you been smuggling over the border?"

18) A woman frantically rushed her daughter's goldfish to the vet. It was alive, but barely. It was floating listlessly and only moved when it absolutely had to. "Please help me," she begged. "My daughter's fish is dying and she loves it so much! She'll be heartbroken if he dies."

The vet assured her all would be well, told her to leave the fish with him and to come back in an hour.

When the woman returns the fish has gone from barely breathing to swimming around the bowl, happy and healthy.

How did the vet manage this miracle?

19) Billy is four years old and sadly, both his parents have died. His guardian loved him but just could not care for little Billy. She found him a new home in the country, bid him farewell, and put him on a train. Since Billy could not read or write, his guardian tied a large tag around his neck with the address to his new home. However, in spite of the clearly stated address on his neck and the watchfulness of the train staff, poor little Billy never makes it to his new home. Why didn't he make it?

20) A lady approaches a man behind a counter. She hands him a book, he looks at it and says, "That will be $3.50, please." She smiles, hands him the money, then turns and leaves without the book. He sees her leave so he knows she does not have it but he does nothing about it. Why?

Rebus Puzzles, Ciphers, and Word Scrambles For Everyone

Rebus Puzzles

A Rebus puzzle is a picture made up of letters or words that represent phrases, words, or sayings. It takes a sharp mind to find the meanings hidden in these unique puzzles!

1) IMPORTANT = IMPORTANT

2) u r YY 4 me

3) ONCE
    T
    I
    M
    E

4) Mount
   Mount
   Mount
   Mount
   Mount
   Mount
   Mount
   Mount
   Mount
   Mount

5) A (4) ID

6) Gra(v)ity

7) ◆ ○

Ciphers (Cryptology)

Cryptology is the use of ciphers and codes to hide or "encrypt" messages to conceal their true meanings and origins. Ciphers can range from highly sophisticated like you might find in military or covert operations to the more simple and fun versions that we will explore here. There are too many types of ciphers to try them all, but here are a few examples of some simpler and enjoyable ones.

Caesar Cipher: The Caesar Cipher is one of the easiest to crack. It is a type of "substitution cipher" that replaces each letter of the coded message with a substitute letter. That substitute is a fixed number of positions farther down in the alphabet. Decipher this message:

Urvhv duh uhg

Key: Letters are shifted 3 places down/forward the alphabet from originals

Atbash Cipher: The Atbash Cipher is much more specific. This cipher reverses the letters of the alphabet. For example, A becomes Z, B becomes Y, etc.
See if you can decipher this message:

"Orev uli glwzb."

Keyword Cipher:

The Keyword Cipher is actually identical to the Caesar Cipher except you choose a word for the substitution alphabet. In order to use this cipher, you must write down the letters of the alphabet then directly underneath it, write the keyword you have chosen plus the remaining letters (the ones not used in the keyword). To *encipher* the message you convert the letters in the top row alphabet to the corresponding letters directly below:

ABCDEFGHIJKLMNOPQRSTUVWXYZ
GOLDENABCFHIJKMPQRSTUVWXYZ

As you can see in this example, the keyword is GOLDEN. Using this key, see if you can ***encipher*** this phrase:

"Fourscore and seven years ago..."

Word Scrambles

Word scrambles are just plain fun! They can be as easy or as complicated as you want and they never seem to get old. See if you can unscramble these eggs!

1) A B C D E I N R S T U

2) C I A D C N E L A T

3) E S I L M

4) O R C U S H T I P

5) B T E L E E

6) R K O F

7) M T P E L E

8) O M E N Y

9) K E C A

10) U F B F L A O

Chapter 4: Megamind Level

Now since you've made to this far, congratulations! You Have Successfully learned different ways and perspectives to think about a situation. So let's play the big game. I have introduced this pattern because a lot of people get bored solving same types of problems and riddles so for keeping the interest alive in solving teasers, this chapter includes **Random Brain Teasers** of different types. This Is A Elite Level. Enjoy!

P.S.- Some Of the teasers in this chapter might be difficult to solve or grasp, children can skip them!

So Let's Find Out, If You Are Smart Enough Hmm.?

Logic, Math, Who Am I?, Rebus Puzzles, Quiz, Word scrambles, Ciphers.

1) You are on an island in the middle of a lake. The lake is in a remote part of the country and there has never been a bridge connecting the island to the mainland. Every day a tractor and wagon gives hay rides around the island. Puzzled as to how the tractor had gotten onto the island, you ask around and find out that the tractor was not transported to the island by boat or by air. Nor was it built on the island. Explain how the tractor got there?

Hint: when everyone feels cold and water gets frozen.

2) You are standing next to a well, and you have two jugs. One jug has a content of 3 liters and the other one has a content of 5 liters.

How can you get just 4 liters of water using only these two jugs?

3) S T A 4 N C E   (Rebus)

4) S D R G M L B E C E A G S   (Word scramble)

5) I am something people love or hate. I change people's appearances and thoughts. If a person takes care of them self I will go up even higher. To some people I will fool them. To others I am a mystery. Some people might want to try and hide me but I will show. No matter how hard people try I will never go down. What am I?

6) Flat as a leaf, round as a ring; has two eyes, can't see a thing. What is it?

7) The following brain teaser has been shared more than 3 million times on Facebook. It seems to be easy for some people but difficult for others. Which group are you in?

6 + 4 = 210

9 + 2 = 711

8 + 5 = 313

5 + 2 = 37

7 + 6 = 113

9 + 8 = 117

10 + 6 = 416

15 + 3 = 1218

?? + ?? = 123

8) Who makes it, has no need of it. Who buys it, has no use for it. Who uses it can neither see nor feel it. What is it?

9) Forward I am heavy, but backward I am not. What am I?

10) What is as light as a feather, but even the world's strongest man couldn't hold it for more than a minute?

11) Atbash Cipher

ZGGZXP ZG WZDM

Key: A is Z and Z is A.

12) **Einstein's riddle**: It is said that this quiz was made up by the famous physicist and according to him 98% will not solve it.

There is a row of five different color houses. Each house is occupied by a man of different nationality. Each man has a different pet, prefers a different drink, and smokes different brand of cigarettes.

1. The Brit lives in the Red house.
2. The Swede keeps dogs as pets.
3. The Dane drinks tea.
4. The Green house is next to the White house, on the left.
5. The owner of the Green house drinks coffee.
6. The person who smokes Pall Mall rears birds.
7. The owner of the Yellow house smokes Dunhill.
8. The man living in the center house drinks milk.
9. The Norwegian lives in the first house.
10. The man who smokes blends lives next to the one who keeps cats.
11. The man who keeps horses lives next to the man who smokes Dunhill.
12. The man who smokes Blue Master drinks beer.

13. The German smokes Prince.
14. The Norwegian lives next to the Blue house.
15. The man who smokes Blends has a neighbor who drinks water.
    Who has fish at home? Are you one of the 2%?

13) **Alphametic puzzles** (also called cryptarithms) are arithmetic problems which involve words where each letter stands for unique digit that makes the arithmetic equation true. For instance, this is one of the famous equations. Can you solve it?

ALFA + BETA + GAMA = DELTA

14) Adam has none, Eve has two, Everyone else has five. What is it that they have?

15) Use the 10 letters A C D E H I J L N P to spell out the names of four countries. Each name must be five letters long, and the four countries must be neighbors.

16) Having 2 sand-glasses: one 7-minute and the second one 4-minute, how can you correctly time 9 minutes?

17) A basket contains 5 apples. Do you know how to divide them among 5 kids so that each one has an apple and one apple stays in the basket?

18) A NE FRIEND ED   (Rebus)

19) VA DERS   (Rebus)

20) You can drop me from the tallest building and I'll be fine, but if you drop me in water I die. What am I?

21) What has a head and a tail, but no body?

22) **Keyword Cipher**

Decipher the following code using principles of keyword cipher taught in previous lesson.

Onqsml Qnbifld Tefs Fs Vnqy Fltnjjfdnlt

Key: BRAIN

23) **Surprising Sequence**   2 9 3 1 8 4 3 6 5 7

What is the next term in this sequence?

24) Lighter than what I am made of, More of me is hidden than is seen. What am I?

25) What kind of room has no doors or windows?

26) Imagine you are in a dark room. How do you get out?

27) What is at the end of a rainbow?

28) One chicken lays two eggs in three days. How many eggs do three chickens lay in nine days?

29) Give 100 meaningful words in one and half minutes without having an "A" in spelling.

30) Martin has one of the numbers 1, 2, or 3 in mind. Sophie is allowed to ask one question to Martin to find out which of these three numbers he has in mind. Martin will answer this question only with the answers "yes", "no", or "I don't know".
The question: Which question should Sophie ask Martin to find out in one time which number he has in mind?

31) You are travelling in a electric train at 60 miles/hour to south, if you are sitting faced towards north, In what direction the engine smoke is flowing?

32) **Mental Arithmetic Test**

Perform the calculation below as fast as you can, and using only mental arithmetic (so without pen and paper, or a calculator!).

Take 1000 and add 40.
Add 1000.
Add 30 and then add 1000.
Add 20.
Add 1000 and then add 10.

The question: What is the result of this calculation?

33) **Knights, Knaves and Normals**

Imagine you are on an island called Texel, with inhabitants that look the same from the outside, but differ in their truthfulness. We distinguish the following types:
- Knights, who always tell the truth.
- Knaves, who never tell the truth.
- Normals, who sometimes tell the truth and sometimes lie.

Assume you meet one of these inhabitants, and he tells you: *"I'm no Knight"*. Then, of what type is inhabitant?

    a) Knight
    b) Knave
    c) Normal
    d) Indeterminable

34) A certain street contains 100 buildings. They are numbered from 1 to 100. How many times does the digit 9 occur in these numbers?

    a) 10
    b) 11
    c) 19
    d) 20

35) One day Alice meets the Lion and the Unicorn in the Forest of Forgetfulness. She knows that the Lion lies on Mondays, Tuesdays, and Wednesdays, and tells the truth on the other days of the week. The Unicorn, on the other hand, lies on

Thursdays, Fridays, and Saturdays, but tells the truth on the other days of the week.

Now they make the following statements to Alice:
    Lion: Yesterday was one of my lying days.
    Unicorn: Yesterday was one of my lying days too.

What day is it?
    a) Sunday
    b) Monday
    c) Tuesday
    d) Wednesday
    e) Thursday
    f) Friday
    g) Saturday

36) I have many feathers to help me fly. I have a body and head, but I'm not alive. It is your strength which determines how far I go. You can hold me in your hand, but I'm never thrown. What am I?

37) You are walking through a field, and you find something to eat. It doesn't have bones, and it doesn't have meat. You pick it

up and put it into your pocket. You take it home and put it on a shelf, but 3 days later it walks away. What is it?

38) How much dirt is in a hole that is 3 ft. deep, and 6 inches in diameter?

39) An old man wanted to leave all of his money to one of his three sons, but he didn't know which one he should give it to. He gave each of them a few coins and told them to buy something that would be able to fill their living room. The first man bought straw, but there was not enough to fill the room. The second bought some sticks, but they still did not fill the room. The third man bought two things that filled the room, so he obtained his father's fortune. What were the two things that the man bought?

40) Two men are in a desert. They both have backpacks on. One of the guys is dead. The guy who is alive has his backpack open, the guy who is dead has his backpack closed. What is in the backpack?

41) A man was outside taking a walk when it began to rain. He did not have an umbrella and he wasn't wearing a hat. His

clothes were soaked, yet not a single hair on his head got wet. How could this happen?

42) What is it that is shiny but deaf, dumb and blind and always tells the truth?

43) There are 20 people in an empty, square room. Each person has full sight of the entire room and everyone in it without turning his head or body, or moving in any way (other than the eyes). Where can you place an apple so that all but one person can see it?

44) One big hockey fan claimed to be able to tell the score before any game. How did he do it?

45) When is a man drowned, but still not wet?

Chapter 5: Bonus Level

Most things we use today were invented by scientists. Inventions are creations of new devices (or processes) as a result from study and experimentation by mostly scientists. This part is included especially for children but adults also can take away fun from this. Do you know which scientist is credited for which invention?

1) This person is associated with the invention or discovery of what?

Mikhail Kalashnikov

    a) Mechanical printing
    b) X-ray machine
    c) AK-47 assault rifle
    d) Telephone

2) Which person is associated with this invention or discovery?

Telephone

    a) John Pemberton
    b) Karl Benz
    c) Samuel Morse
    d) Alexander Graham Bell

3) Which person is associated with this invention or discovery?

Vulcanization of rubber

- a) Charles Goodyear
- b) Alexander Fleming
- c) Laszlo Biro
- d) J. Robert Oppenheimer

4) Which person is associated with this invention or discovery?

Modern ballpoint pen

- a) Alexander Fleming
- b) John Harvey Kellogg
- c) Laszlo Biro
- d) Montgolfier brothers

5) Which person is associated with this invention or discovery?

Petrol-powered automobile

- a) Charles Goodyear
- b) Johann Gutenberg
- c) Karl Benz
- d) Alessandro Volta

6) Which person is associated with this invention or discovery?

Electric Guitar

a) Edward Jenner
b) Les Paul
c) Samuel Colt
d) Alexander G. Bell

7) Which person is associated with this invention or discovery?

Coca-Cola

a) Thomas Edison
b) John Pemberton
c) Alfred Nobel
d) George Eastman

8) Which person is associated with this invention or discovery?

Roll film

a) George Eastman
b) Wilhelm Conrad Rontgen
c) John Moses Browning
d) Levi Strauss

9) Which person is associated with this invention or discovery?

Hot-air balloon

a) Montgolfier brothers
b) Isaac Singer
c) Dmitri Mendeleev
d) John Harvey Kellogg

10) Which person is associated with this invention or discovery?

Penicillin

a) Alexander Fleming
b) Wilhelm Conrad Rontgen
c) John Moses Browning
d) Levi Strauss

11) Which person is associated with this invention or discovery?

World Wide Web [WWW]

a) Karl Benz
b) Tim Berners-Lee
c) Charles Macintosh
d) John Harvey Kellogg

12) Which person is associated with this invention or discovery?

Mechanical printing

   a) Johann Gutenberg
   b) Tim Berners-Lee
   c) Charles Macintosh
   d) Wilhelm Conrad Rontgen

13) Which person is associated with this invention or discovery?

Powered airplane

   a) Wilhelm Conrad Rontgen
   b) Orville and Wilbur Wright
   c) Alfred Nobel
   d) Nikola Tesla

14) Which person is associated with this invention or discovery?

Bifocal glasses

   a) Laszlo Biro
   b) Thomas Edison
   c) Benjamin Franklin
   d) Charles Macintosh

15) Which person is associated with this invention or discovery?

Helicopter

a) Alfred Nobel
b) George Eastman
c) Thomas Edison
d) Igor Sikorsky

16) Which person is associated with this invention or discovery?

Barometer

a) Alfred Nobel
b) George Eastman
c) Thomas Edison
d) Blaise Pascal

17) Which person is associated with this invention or discovery?

Phonograph

a) Thomas Edison
b) Charles Macintosh
c) Laszlo Biro
d) Guglielmo Marconi

18) Which person is associated with this invention or discovery?

Induction motor

a) Isaac Singer

b) Samuel Morse
c) Nikola Tesla
d) Charles Goodyear

19) Which person is associated with this invention or discovery?

Periodic table

a) Mikhail Kalashnikov
b) Dmitri Mendeleev
c) Johann Gutenberg
d) Levi Strauss

20) Which person is associated with this invention or discovery?

First successful machine gun

a) Benjamin Franklin
b) Wilhelm Conrad Rontgen
c) Charles Goodyear
d) Richard J. Gatling & Hiram S. Maxim

21) Which person is associated with this invention or discovery?

Levi's Jeans Fabric

a) Charles Macintosh

b) Levi Strauss

c) Jacob Davis

d) Stephanie Louise Kwolek

22) Which person is associated with this invention or discovery?

Telegraph

a) Samuel Morse

b) Johann Gutenberg

c) Dmitri Mendeleev

d) Mikhail Kalashnikov

23) Which person is associated with this invention or discovery?

Dynamite

a) Alfred Nobel

b) Johann Gutenberg

c) Dmitri Mendeleev

d) Mikhail Kalashnikov

24) Which person is associated with this invention or discovery?

Cornflake breakfasts

a) Orville and Wilbur Wright

b) Guglielmo Marconi

c) John Harvey Kellogg

d) Nikola Tesla

25) Which person is associated with this invention or discovery?

Commercially practical light bulb

a) William Kennedy Laurie Dickson
b) Thomas Edison
c) Peter Carl Goldmark
d) John Napier

26) Which person is associated with this invention or discovery?

Hovercraft

a) Charles Macintosh
b) William Murdoch
c) Christopher Cockerell
d) Robert Adler

27) Which person is associated with this invention or discovery?

Electric sewing machine

a) Peter Carl Goldmark
b) Philip Diehl

c) Eli Whitney
d) Percy Spencer

28) Which person is associated with this invention or discovery?

Magnetic Tape

e) Whitcomb Judson
f) Samuel Colt
g) Fritz Pfleumer
h) Felix Hoffmann (Bayer)

29) Which person is associated with this invention or discovery?

Holography

a) Les Paul
b) Dennis Gabor
c) Yoshiro Nakamatsu
d) James Naismith

30) Which person is associated with this invention or discovery?

Pendulum clock

a) Dennis Gabor
b) Peter Carl Goldmark

c) Douglas Engelbart

d) Christiaan Huygens

31) Which person is associated with this invention or discovery?

Bacteria

a) Clarence Birdseye

b) Christiaan Huygens

c) Roger Bacon

d) Antoine van Leeuwenhoek

32) Which person is associated with this invention or discovery?

Stethoscope

a) Auguste and Louis Lumiere

b) Peter Carl Goldmark

c) Rene Laennec

d) Percy Spencer

33) Which person is associated with this invention or discovery?

The computer mouse

a) Thomas Edison

b) James Naismith
c) Whitcomb Judson
d) Douglas Engelbart

34) Which person is associated with this invention or discovery?

Motion picture camera

a) Felix Hoffmann (Bayer)
b) Clarence Birdseye
c) William Kennedy Laurie Dickson
d) Percy Spencer

35) Which person is associated with this invention or discovery?

Optical character recognition and flatbed scanner

a) Rene Laennec
b) Raymond Kurzweil
c) William Kennedy Laurie Dickson
d) Dennis Gabor

36) Which person is associated with this invention or discovery?

Dishwasher

a) Charles Macintosh
b) James Hargreaves
c) Felix Hoffmann (Bayer)
d) Josephine Cochrane

37) Which person is associated with this invention or discovery?

Zipper

a) Samuel Colt
b) Whitcomb Judson
c) Felix Hoffmann (Bayer)
d) Eli Whitney

38) Which person is associated with this invention or discovery?

Nuclear model of an Atom

a) Percy Spencer
b) Ernest Rutherford
c) Whitcomb Judson
d) Charles Macintosh

39) Which person is associated with this invention or discovery?

Modern frozen food industry

a) Les Paul

b) James Hargreaves
c) Ernest Rutherford
d) Clarence Birdseye

40) Which person is associated with this invention or discovery?

Revolver gun

a) William Kennedy Laurie Dickson
b) Josephine Cochrane
c) Eli Whitney
d) Samuel Colt

41) Which person is associated with this invention or discovery?

Piano

a) Samuel Guthrie
b) Thomas Edison
c) William George Armstrong
d) Bartolomeo Cristofori

42) Which person is associated with this invention or discovery?

Chocolate milk

a) Stephanie Kwolek

b) Edwin H. Armstrong
c) Herman Hollerith
d) Coenraad Johannes van Houten

43) Which person is associated with this invention or discovery?

LED (Light Emitting Diode)

a) Nick Holonyak
b) Eugen Baumann
c) Theophilus Van Kannel
d) Robert Goddard

44) Which person is associated with this invention or discovery?

FM radio

a) Bartolomeo Cristofori
b) Edwin H. Armstrong
c) Theophilus Van Kannel
d) Thomas Edison

45) Which person is associated with this invention or discovery?

The modern fire extinguisher

a) George William Manby

b) Edwin Beard Budding
c) Arthur Wynne
d) Coenraad Johannes van Houten

46) Which person is associated with this invention or discovery?

Eau de Cologne

a) Nick Holonyak
b) Stephanie Kwolek
c) Coenraad Johannes van Houten
d) Johann Maria Farina

47) Which person is associated with this invention or discovery?

Spinning jenny

a) Rene Laennec
b) Eli Whitney
c) Fritz Pfleumer
d) James Hargreaves

48) Which of these men invented the game of basketball?

a) Walter Camp
b) James Naismith
c) James G. Creighton

d) William G. Morgan

49) Which person is associated with this invention or discovery?

Logarithms

    a) Samuel Colt
    b) John Napier
    c) Felix Hoffmann (Bayer)
    d) Whitcomb Judson

50) Which person is associated with this invention or discovery?

Aspirin

    a) Thomas Edison
    b) Dennis Gabor
    c) Felix Hoffmann (Bayer)
    d) Fritz Pfleumer

51) The Niepce Crater on the Moon was named in recognition of the famous inventor Joseph Niepce. What did Niepce invent?

    a) A telescope.
    b) A camera.

c) A microscope.
d) A Magnifier

52) Who invented the television?

a) John Baird.
b) Philo Farnsworth.
c) Vladimir Zworykin.
d) Both Philo Farnsworth and Vladimir Zworykin

53) This famous inventor was considered to be far ahead of his time. He recorded his inventions in journals. Many of these inventions did not become known until centuries later. Who was this inventor?

a) Galileo Galilei.
b) Leonardo da Vinci.
c) Nostradamus.
d) Archimedes

54) Marion Donovan made life easier for mothers by inventing what?

a) The disposable diaper
b) The baby carriage
c) Baby wipes
d) Pacifiers

55) Who took the world's first photograph?

  a) George Eastman
  b) Edwin Land
  c) Joseph Niepce
  d) Guglielmo Marconi

56) Who developed the first modern automobile?

  a) Henry Ford
  b) Karl Benz
  c) Nils Bohlin
  d) Robert Fulton

57) What Galileo invented?

  a) Barometer
  b) Pendulum clock
  c) Microscope
  d) Thermometer

58) What J. B. Dunlop invented?

  a) Pneumatic rubber tire
  b) Automobile wheel rim
  c) Rubber boot
  d) Model airplanes

59) Who is the creator of the Nobel Prizes, including that of Peace, also invented?
Dynamite.

   a) Marie and Pierre Curie
   b) Thomas A Edison
   c) Albert Einstein
   d) Alfred Nobel

60) This statesman, politician, scholar, inventor, and one of early presidents of USA invented the swivel chair, the spherical sundial, the moldboard plow, and the cipher wheel.

   a) George Washington
   b) Alexander Hamilton
   c) John Adams
   d) Thomas Jefferson

Hints

Beginner Level Hints

23) "Smooth and turbulent" is your clue.

24) This word means "nothing inside."

25) This one is a bit of a "reach."

29) You'll have to "single" this answer out.

30) You'll find this person crunching numbers in almost every office.

33) It's all in a name.

36) Don't overthink "opposite."

Pro Level Hints

1) You don't need a hint for this one! I'm sure you'll get it right.

2) Yours is mine and mine is yours.

3) There's a lot of "flipping" going on here.

4) There is one question where the truth will be the same as the lie.

5) This one is tough. Like the eggs and the hourglass, there is a lot of back and forth. You just have to figure out the math!

6) Another tough one! You have to figure out the math. One hint: two of the children are the same age.

7) The one's place in the answer must be "zero."

8) Some of the men have two roles.

9) There was something the man did that he shouldn't have needed to do.

10) Wood comes in many forms.

12) Don't forget about the fractions.

13) It's all in the "past."

14) Keep in mind that the other princes are very smart and the king promised   that the test was fair. There are no tricks involved, just deductive reasoning.

15) He only knows what he sees.

16) You don't need to see the coins to make this happen.

20) There are no reflective surfaces, no trick questions or wording. The Guru is not seeking out any one individual.

22) Think "legs."

25) This is a tricky question!

33) The answer is a little tricky this "time."

35) I rhyme with eleven.

40) Only *one* is not a nickel.

Expert Level Hints

1) This hint is more of a "tip."

3) Feel the heat.

5) There is also a puddle of water on the floor.

6) It's a bit "frosty" out there too.

8) The men have a history together.

9) It has to do with what they never were.

10) It's all about love.

11) Ladies like poker too.

17) How does he get from point A to point B?

Answers

Beginner Level Answers

1) Candle

2) It's a one-story house. There are no stairs!

3) A clock

4) A towel

5) All of them!

6) He was bald.

7) The horse's name was Friday.

8) The surgeon was his mother.

9) You took away 2, so you have 2.

10) Dana, of course!

11) He threw it straight up in the air.

12) The doorbell

13) A needle

14) Wrong

15) A bottle

16) Nothing

17) A piano

18) I am a glove

19) The letter M

20) Stars

21) A keyboard

22) A shadow

23) The ocean

24) Empty! (mpty, emty, emp-t, m t)

25) The man is a midget.

26) Ice!

27) A map

28) The letter "R"

29) The passengers are all married.

30) Bookkeeper

31) Silence

32) They are standing back-to-back.

33) The magician had written "your actual name"

34) Ad-dress

35) Her daughter!

36) They were already facing each other.

37) Just one

38) A stamp

39) A secret

40) A reflection

Pro Level Answers

1) The door to the right cause a tiger that hasn't eaten in 3 months is most likely dead!

2) The wise man told them to switch horses because "technically" the will stated that the owner the of slowest horse would get the inheritance. So if one son beat his brother who was riding his horse, he would win.

3) Turn both hourglasses once you start the egg. When the 7-minute runs out, turn it back over. Once the1-minute one is out in 4 minutes, turn it over once more. It will take the same 4 minutes to run out, giving your egg the5 minutes it needs to boil.

4) He must ask each one "What path would your brother tell me to take?" They will both say the same thing, which means the traveler must take the opposite path to eternal happiness. (The liar would answer "my brother would say to take the right path". His brother knows he will lie so he answers the same.)

5) Yes, exactly5 minutes:

a) Persons and 2 cross together and brings the light back, taking 3 minutes
b) Then 3 and 4 cross the bridge and 2 brings the light back, taking up another0 minutes

c) Lastly, and 2 go back across the bridge together with the torch taking up the remaining 2 minutes

6) Their ages are 3,3, and 8. After looking at his house number, she would know the sum of their ages. There are only 2 sets of numbers that share a sum that can be multiplied together to reach 72: 2, 6, 6, and 3, 3, and 8. After being told his *oldest* child liked chocolate pudding, it was clear which set of numbers indicated an obvious oldest child: 3,3, and 8.

7) Keeping in mind that the one's place in the answer (1,000) must be zero, here is the equation of 8's: 888+88+8+8+8=1000.

8) It is a grandfather, his son, and his son's son eating breakfast. The grandfather and his son make 2 fathers, and the father and his son make 2 sons, so two fathers and two sons, but there are still only 3 people at the table.

9) No one knocks on his or her own hotel room door. He would have tried his key first.

10) The man was carrying sawdust.

11) He sent1 cartons total: 7 large boxes (7x8=56), 4 small boxes (4x10=40). So 96 boxes that fit into1 cartons.

12) He never actually makes it to the one-foot mark since distance is taken away each jump he makes.

13) Only six. Elise *had* (past tense) 2 kids, indicating that she no longer has them.

14) You are also wearing a white hat. The king promised that the test would be fair. If you were wearing a black hat while the other two were white, only two princes would be able to see the difference in colors, leaving you at a disadvantage. Plus, if you were the only one wearing a black hat, it would not take very long for one of the other princes to figure out he was wearing a white one. Being an intelligent person looking at a black hat and a white hat, he would realize that a just king would never pick 2 black hats and a white one, which would mean his own was white. And if he was seeing two black hats he would instantly know he was wearing white. Therefore, the only way the test can be as fair as the king swears it is if all princes are wearing the same color, and there are 3 white hats.

15) The one who stopped would've asked himself what the others had seen that was so funny. If he (being the smartest philosopher) had nothing on his head, which meant that the second smartest philosopher would have soon figured out that the third smartest was only laughing at the second smartest man so then the second smartest philosopher would have stopped laughing.

16) Put them into two sets of0. Each set would then have an equal number of heads and tails.

17) If they're both at the park, then they're both the same distance from the school!

18) The people simply miscalculated. The error is in them adding the $27 and the $2. The $2 is actually the change of the change, *not* the true change in this transaction.
The three people paid $30 between them and they were given $5 back as change, but $2 gets returned to the establishment. In the end, they have paid a total of $27: $30-$5+$2= $27. Factor in the $3 change that they actually kept and it brings it back to $30.

19) They both have the same amount again! You've replaced the spoonful you took out of the lemonade glass when you put the spoonful of the ink/lemonade mixture back into the lemonade glass.

20) The answer is 100 days after the Guru says this, all of the 100 people with blue eyes will leave on the 100th day. Here are the theories of the logic behind the answer:

1) **If there is one blue-eyed person, he/she leaves that first night.** If you consider the possibility that there is just one blue-eyed person on the island, he

would obviously know he's the only one the Guru could be talking about since he can see everyone else's eyes. He would then leave on the ferry that first night.

2) If there are 2 people with blue eyes, they will both leave that night. So, in this case, two people with blue eyes will look at each other and think "if my eyes aren't blue then that person has the only blue eyes. They'll both wait, realize neither one of them are trying to leave and so arrive at the conclusion that they both have blue eyes and they both leave on the ferry the second night.

And then consider three blue-eyed people, then four, and so on and so on until theory 99 is reached. The logic is the same, and by the time the 99th day has passed, all100 blue-eyed people now know they have blue eyes so they will all leave on the 100th night.

(Here is the link to the riddle if there are any more questions or confusion: https://xkcd.com/solution.html)

21) The cell phone cost $105, the case cost $5 totaling $110.

22) They are getting $4.50 per leg, so the cat would get $18.

23) None! Roosters don't lay eggs!

24) There are 977 remaining animals. (Equation: 100x2= 200; Two pairs to each original equals to 4 animals= 800; 200+800=1,000;,1000-23= 977).

25) Nine! (all but 9, get smashed and ruined).

26) None, the barn is already built!

27)100 eggs. At $0.12 a dozen, that is one cent per egg; dollar is 100 cents and can buy 100 eggs.

28) The glasses cost $15.50.

29) She had $0.25 left (one of the quarters).

30) 1/6th of 30 in the alien land is 6.

31) Zero!

32) Nine.

33) If you add 5 hours to 9 am you get 2 pm!

34) They both weigh a ton.

35) Seven (take away the "S" to make "even")

36) One! Once you put an egg in it, it's not empty anymore.

37) There are 20 nines.

38) They cost the same!

39) Because if it was one inch longer it would be a foot!

40) A fifty-cent piece and a nickel. The phrase "one is not a nickel" is only true about one of the coins, meaning the other one could be!

Expert Level Answers

1) All they have to do is tip the barrel until the cider touches the rim. If the bottom is exposed, it's less than half full.

2) The same person served as president for 2 different terms (just not consecutively).

3) Flip the first switch, leave it on for about one minute, then turn it off. Flip the second one on then walk into the room. The second light will be on and the first bulb will still be warm. Find the warm one and you will know which bulb the 3rd switch turns on.

4) The match, obviously!

5) He threw the rope up into the rafters, put it around his neck, and then stood on a 3-foot high block of ice. Once the ice melted, he was hung.

6) The items had been used on a snowman that has now melted.

7) They were, in fact, only two of four, making them quadruplets, not twins!

8) The three men knew each other and had once been shipwrecked on a desert island. In their desperation for food, they made a pact: they would cut off their left arms to eat rather than eating each other. One of the men was a doctor so he cut off the arms of his friends. And then, in a cruel twist of irony, they were rescued. Their oath was binding, however, and the doctor followed through by having his arm amputated and sent to his island companions.

9) Neither Adam nor Eve had been conceived and born the conventional human way. So they were the only ones there with no belly buttons!

10) Mindy helps the old woman into the passenger seat of her car, gives her keys to her old friend and waits for the bus with her soul mate.

11) The fireman is the only man in the room and the police knew the suspect's name was "Mike."

12) The last person took the whole plate with the egg on it so it was technically still on the plate.

13) It was daytime!

14) Candy say down in the chair and Mandy ran around it twice then said: "I'll come back in a month and run around the third time!"

15) None. The tree will not produce any plums seeing as it is a pear tree!

16) The glass was empty.

17) The man is smuggling motorcycles.

18) The vet uses the hour to run out and buy a new goldfish!

19) "Billy" is, in fact, a "Billy" goat. He ate the tag with the address on it so no one knew where he was going.

20) Because it was an overdue library book.

Rebus Puzzle Answers

1) It means one thing is equally as important as another.

2) You are too wise for me...[2 Ys]

3) Once upon a time (because the "once" sits on top of "time")

4) "Mount"0 times = "mountain"

5) 4 in AID = foreign aid.

6) (v) is the center of gravity = Center of gravity.

7) It's a diamond ring.

Cipher Answers

1) Roses are red

2) "Live for today."

3) "Nmurslmre gkd sevek yegrs gam..."

Word Scramble Answers

1) Disturbance

2) Accidental

3) Slime

4) Courtship

5) Beetle

6) Fork

7) Temple

8) Money

9) Cake

10) Buffalo

Megamind Level Answers

Logic, Math, Who Am I?, Rebus Puzzles, Quiz, Word scrambles, Cipher Answers

1) It was driven over in winter, when the lake was frozen.

2) Solution:
Fill the 5-liter jug. Then fill the 3-liter jug to the top with water from the 5-liter jug. Now you have 2 liters of water in the 5-liter jug. Dump out the 3-liter jug and pour what is in the 5-liter jug into the 3-liter jug. Then refill the 5-liter jug, and fill up the 3-liter jug to the top. Since there were already 2 liters of water in the 3-liter jug, liter is removed from the 5-liter jug, leaving 4 liters of water in the 5-liter jug.

Solution 2:
Fill the 3-liter jug and pour it into the 5-liter jug. Then refill the 3-liter jug and fill up the 5-liter jug to the top. Since there were already 3 liters of water in the 5-liter jug, 2 liters of water are removed from the 3-liter jug, leaving liter of water in the 3-liter jug. Then dump out the 5-liter jug and pour what is in the 3-liter jug into the 5-liter jug. Refill the 3-liter jug and pour it into the 5-liter jug. Now you have 4 liters of water in the 5-liter jug.

3) For Instance. (Four in Stance).

4) SCRAMBBLED EGGS

5) Age.

6) A Button.

7) Split the resulting number "123" into 2 parts - and 23. Those numbers will be 2 results. "1" will be result of "first number minus second number". "23" will be result of "first number plus second number".

So it's easy to see that those 2 numbers will be 12 and 11.
12 -11 = 1
12 +11 = 23
Write them together and you get 23.
So the answer is 12+11 =23.
Was it hard?

8) A coffin.

9) Forward I am ton, backwards I am not.

10) His Breath.

11) Attack At Dawn

ABCDEFGHIJKLMNOPQRSTUVWXYZ

ZYXWVUTSRQPONMLKJIHGFEDCBA

To decipher a message, Find 'Z' in the bottom row, which is 'A' in the top row. Match the letters, Continue until the whole message is deciphered.

12) The Germans Have The Fish.
    Following is the elaboration of riddle.

Norwegian	yellow	Dunhill	water	cat
Dane	blue	Blend	tea	horse
Briton	red	Pall Mall	milk	bird
German	green	Prince	coffee	fish
Swedish	white	Blue Master	beer	dog

13) 5795 + 6435 + 2505 =4735

OR
     5305 + 2475 + 6595 =4375

There are lots of solutions for this problem. The only thing that is fixed is that E=4, A=5

F+M must equal to nine so (F,M) can be from the set (0,9)(1,8)(2,7)(3,6)(4,5)(5,4)(6,3)(9,0)

T can be any digit from 0-9

L can be any digit from 0-9

D can be either or 2

if D=2 then B=G=9

if D=1 then (B,G) can be any combination from the set (0,8)(2,6)(3,5)(4,4)(5,3)(6,2)(8,0)

By following these rules you can simply select random pieces and they are solutions to ALFA+BETA+GAMA=DELTA

14) The Letter 'e'.
Adam has no 'e', Eve has two 'e's and everyone else has 5 'e's.

15) China, Japan, Nepal, India.

16) Turn both sand-glasses. After 4 minutes turn upside down the 4-min sand-glass. When the 7-min sand-glass spills the last grain, turn the 7-min upside down. Then you have minute in the 4-min sand-glass left and after spilling everything, in the 7-min sand-glass there will be minute of sand down (already spilt). Turn the 7-min sand-glass upside down and let the minute go back. And that's it. 4 +3 +1 +1 = 9
Was It Too Hard?

17) 4 kids get an apple (one apple for each one of them) and the fifth kid gets an apple with the basket still containing the apple.

18) A Friend In Need.

19) Space In-vaders.

20) A Paper.

21) A Coin.

22) Person Reading This Is Very Intelligent!!!

Decryption Key:
ABCDEFGHIJKLMNOPQRSTUVWXYZ
BRAINCDEFGHJKLMOPQSTUVWXYZ

23) **Surprising Sequence**

This single sequence in fact consists of two sequences: the first sequence is 2-3-4-5-... and the second sequence is 9-18-36-72-... . To make the puzzle harder, all digits have been placed apart.
OR

Every two consecutive digits in series (1-9) have digits summing to 9 e.g. 2&3 have 9 in between, 3&4 have 8 and 1 in between and 4&5 have 6 and 3 in between, so on...
Conclusion: The next term in the sequence is a "2".

24) An Iceberg.

25) A Mushroom.

26) Stop Imagining.

27) "W"

28) Chicken lays 2 eggs in 3 days, so 3 chickens lay 3×2=6 eggs in 3 days. In 9 days, these 3 chickens lay 3 times as much eggs as in 3 days.
Conclusion: three chickens lay 3×6=18 eggs in nine days

29) One, Two, Three, Four, Five, Six, Seven, Eight, Nine, Ten... (Up To)..., One Hundred.

30) Sophie could for example ask Martin the following:
"I have the number or 2 in mind. Is the number that you have in mind larger than the number I have in mind?" The answer "yes" means that Martin has the number 3 in mind, "I don't know" means 2, and "no" means 1.

31) The train is Electric, there is No Smoke.

32) 4100.
Most people get 5000 as result, if they perform the calculation as fast as they can. However, the answer is 4100. Because of the hurry, the tens and the hundreds are mixed up in the last step (4090 plus 10).

33) Normal.

A Knight cannot make the statement "I'm no Knight", since this would be a lie and a Knight always tells the truth. A Knave could also not make the statement, since that would be a true statement, and a Knave never tells the truth. A Normal however can say, "I'm no Knight". It is true, and Normals sometimes tell the truth.

34) 20.

Just count the nines in the numbers: 9, 19, 29, 39, 49, 59, 69, 79, 89, 90, 91, 92, 93, 94, 95, 96, 97, 98, and 99.
Note: 99 contains TWO nines!

35) Thursday.

The only days the Lion can say that he lied on the previous day are Mondays and Thursdays.
The only days the Unicorn can say this, are Thursdays and Sundays.
Therefore, the only day they both say that is on Thursday.

36) An Arrow

37) It's an Egg.

38) None. A hole only has air in it, no dirt.

39) His wise son bought a candle and a box of matches. After lighting the candle, the light filled the entire room.

40) A Parachute that didn't open.

41) He was bald.

42) A Mirror.

43) Place the apple on one person's head.

44) The score before any hockey game should be 0:0, shouldn't it?

45) When trapped in quicksand.

Bonus Level Quiz Answer

1) AK-47 assault rifle.

2) Alexander Graham Bell.

3) Charles Goodyear.

4) Laszlo Biro.

5) Karl Benz.

6) Les Paul.

7) John Pemberton.

8) George Eastman.

9) Montgolfier brothers.

10) Alexander Fleming.

11) Tim Berners-Lee.

12) Johann Gutenberg.

13) Orville and Wilbur Wright.

14) Benjamin Franklin.

15) Igor Sikorsky.

16) Blaise Pascal.

17) Thomas Edison.

18) Nikola Tesla.

19) Dmitri Mendeleev.

20) Richard J. Gatling & Hiram S. Maxim.

21) Levi Strauss.

22) Samuel Morse.

23) Alfred Nobel.

24) John Harvey Kellogg.

25) Thomas Edison.

26) Christopher Cockerell.

27) Philip Diehl.

28) Fritz Pfleumer.

29) Dennis Gabor.

30) Christiaan Huygens.

31) Antoine van Leeuwenhoek.

32) Rene Laennec.

33) Douglas Engelbart.

34) William Kennedy Laurie Dickson.

35) Raymond Kurzweil.

36) Josephine Cochrane.

37) Whitcomb Judson.

38) Ernest Rutherford.

39) Clarence Birdseye.

40) Samuel Colt.

41) Bartolomeo Cristofori.

42) Coenraad Johannes van Houten.

43) Nick Holonyak.

44) Edwin H. Armstrong.

45) George William Manby.

46) Johann Maria Farina.

47) James Hargreaves.

48) John Napier.

49) James Naismith.

50) Felix Hoffmann (Bayer).

51) A camera.

52) Both Philo Farnsworth and Vladimir Zworykin.

53) Leonardo da Vinci.

54) The disposable diaper.

55) Joseph Niepce.

56) Karl Benz.

57) Thermometer.

58) Pneumatic rubber tire.

59) Alfred Nobel.

60) Thomas Jefferson.

Conclusion

Thank you for making it through to the end of *The Best Brain Teasers: 199+ Unique Brain Teasers for All Ages*. Let's hope it was informative and able to provide you with all of the tools and inspirations you needed to achieve your goals whatever they may be.

The first step to achieving your goals is understanding how important it is to exercise our brains as much as any other part of the body. Your brain plays a vital role in every decision you take. It doesn't take much time and the lasting benefits to our overall health makes it well worth the effort.

The next step is to put these brain teasers to good use! Riddles are a centuries-old tradition and some riddles have been found actually recorded in ancient civilizations. They teach us critical thinking as well as further developing the ability to look for answers outside of the normal way of thinking. All it takes is a few minutes a day to give our brains the extra attention that they need.

So have some friends over and challenge each other to a riddle duel. Get your family together for some quality time and teach your children the value of using and strengthening their minds. This book has given you the opportunity to have some of the best and most thought-provoking puzzles in one place, making it easy to implement them in your daily life.

*Finally, if you found this book useful in any way, **A review on Amazon** is always appreciated! We Look Forward For Any Suggestions.*

Thank You Again..,

Mike.

Riddles

For

Genius Kids

365 What Am I Riddles,

Brain Teasers And Trick Questions

That Everyone Will Love.

- Mike C. Biehl

Introduction

Kids can't get enough of fun riddles and brain teasers! The **Collection of Riddles For Kids** here is not only fun and engaging, but it will also help to develop your child or student's critical and reasoning skills. Sadly, many kids come to associate learning with boredom, which is a dangerous path for children to begin with. On the other hand, Brain games like riddles, brain teasers, crosswords, trick questions and puzzles are easy, fun and exciting way to make learning and improving one's mind & induce curiosity in young minds. This collection was carefully crafted to provide you with a wide variety of **Riddles and Trick Questions for children** of all ages and abilities.

This **Massive Never Read collection** of riddles, interactive puzzles and trick questions will help you test your child or student's cognitive limits and hone their critical thinking and reasoning skills. Therefore we have created this collection of tricky but fun-engaging riddles for kids for those who enjoy being mentally challenged but also children who need enhancement and improvement in their cognitive abilities. It is always good to challenge the minds of the young to help their brains to develop new neural connections and patterns and confronting children with difficult problems help ready them to deal with the everyday challenges of daily life.

Some of these riddles are easy to solve and some can make you think for hours. Share our riddles with your friends and family. Try some of the hard riddles with your parents and the easy and fun riddles with your younger brothers and sisters. **Laugh, Giggle, And Have Fun.**

Clever Riddles

1)   What two keys can't open any doors?

2)   I have keys but no doors, I have space but no rooms,
     I allow you to enter but you are never able to leave.
     What am I?

3)   After booming and zapping is when I emerge, to
     bring you bright dazzling beauty when I diverge,
     Some say that I hide enormous wealth, but those
     riches have always proven stealth. What am I?

4)   I have wings, I am able to fly, I'm not a bird yet I soar
     high in the sky. What am I?

5)   If four people can repair four bicycles in four hours,
     how many bicycles can eight people repair in eight
     hours?

6) I am used in most sports, have four holes, come in many different colors and there is a state that shares my name. What am I?

7) I am a fruit, I am a bird and I am also a person. What am I?

8) It was a Christmas morning for a family in New York when the mother went to the store, the youngest son was watching SpongeBob Squarepants on TV, the middle son was doing yoga, the eldest son was mowing the lawn, and the father was reading a newspaper. Then, when it was time to eat everyone discovered that all of the food had been eaten. Who ate all the food?

9) What time did the tooth fairy show up to get a kid's tooth and leave a dollar under the pillow?

10) If Santa has reindeers, Charlie Brown has Snoopy and John Arbuckle has Garfield the cat, then what animal would Dracula have?

11) What is always late and never present now?

12) A purple and orange dead butterfly is in the middle of a spider web and all of its legs are caught in the web. The spider notices it and comes running at it ready to tie it up and consume it. If the butterfly wants to get away from a spider, would it have the best chance of survival if it fluttered its wings, wiggled its legs or did both?

13) What do Dalmatians, Lady Bugs, Leopards and Blue (from Blue's Clues) have in common?

14) I come with different colors, I get big when I'm filled, I float away if you don't tie me and I make a sound when I get popped. What am I?

15)   Which one doesn't quite belong: vultures, eagles, hawks, herons, pelicans and ostrich?

16)   Joe, Dennis, Maya, Angel, MJ, Abby, Zoe, Ray, Nicole and Brad were in an airplane crash and every single person died on board. However, when the ambulance arrived they discovered Nicole and Brad still alive. How did this happen?

17)   What is in the middle of bathrooms and will always be in the middle no matter what?

18)   Which one is not white: The White House, white sugar, polar bears and snow?

19)   You keep me close to you and you save me no matter how small or big and dirty I get. What am I?

20)   The little rabbit went outside and ran around in the pouring rain for hours, yet not a single strand of hair got wet. How can this be?

21)   You'll find me in a soup, in a burger, in a pizza, I am green when raw and red when ripened and ready to become a condiment. What am I?

22)   Which weighs more: a ton of concrete or a ton of feathers?

23)   When does April comes before January?

24)   What do Taylor Swift and an air conditioner have in common?

25)   What can you eat, play with, watch with and listen to music to?

26)   Which part of the day is the fastest to break?

27) What do autumn, Halloween, August, and Dracula have in common that a pumpkin doesn't have?

28) 4 rubber ducks were floating in the bathtub, 2 floated away and 2 drowned. How many ducks are still alive?

29) I flicker and I glow and tell stories and put on a show, to make me you must move super-fast many pieces of art from the first to the last. What am I?

30) I can run fast and slow, I can be high or low. I can slip through most anything, and am needed by both the poor and kings. What am I?

31) What do cats, dogs, birds, fish and turtles all have in common?

32) What has feet on the inside but not on the outside?

33)   What is often on the ground getting stepped on by others, but you don't have to wash it because it never get dirty, in fact you couldn't wash it even if you tried?

34)   People usually come see me almost every single day and often many times a day. Despite this, people often consider me to be very dirty. Even though I will never speak to anyone, people will always show me a part of themselves that they rarely show to anyone else. What am I?

35)   Imagine that you are trapped inside a windowless building with nothing but a box of matches, 3 candles and a ceramic mug. The flood waters are rising and are currently up to your neck. The door is hopelessly locked and there is no one within 500 miles of you. How can you get out of this situation?

36)   What word in the dictionary is hilarious?

37)   If 66 = 2, 99 = 2, 888 = 6, 00 = 2, 7777 = 0, 667= 2,
       276 = 1, 833 = 2, then what does 2876 equal?

38)   Sometimes I shine, sometimes I'm dull, sometimes
       I am big, and sometimes I am small. I can be pointy,
       I can be curved, and don't ask me questions because
       even though I'm sharp, I'm not smart enough to
       answer you. What am I?

39)   What do you get if you add 2 blackberries and 5
       apples?

40)   I can be long and can be short, I can be black, white,
       brown or purple. You can find me all over the world
       and I am often the main event. What am I?

41)   What is the equivalent of 4k + 2k +k?

42) You can collect me and you can toss me, you can flip me, you can spin me, and people all around the world have different versions of me. What am I?

43) I am hot, sometimes soft, sometimes hard, sometimes runny and loose, sometimes I float, sometimes I sink but whatever form I take on I always go out and never in. What am I?

44) What did addition say to subtraction when they discovered each other on Facebook?

45) I have branches, sometimes a few and other times hundreds or more, but I have no fruit, trunk or leaves. What am I?

46) What gift should you give blind people, drunks, and nerds for Christmas?

47) If you are in Europe and one of your feet is in Germany while the other is in Belgium, then what country would you really be in?

48) What do Delhi, Mexico, Guinea, Castle, Jersey and Found-land have in common?

49) If Trump and Daisy Duck had a son what would they name him?

50) What did the depressed math book say to the calculator, notebook, and dictionary?

51) What can't you find in European countries like Monaco, Spain, Germany and France that you'll find in Asian countries like, Brunei, Papua New Guinea and Bhutan?

52) How many seconds are there in January?

53) If you find Pope Francis in the Vatican, Kim Jong Un in North Korea and Donald Trump in the United States, then in what country can you find Santa?

54) What did the right eyebrow say to the left eyebrow?

55) I can be sad, I can be happy, I can be angry and cry, I come with many faces and sometimes many sizes and even in disguise of Many Things. I am able to communicate things words often cannot and I can move from place to place at the speed of light. What am I?

56) I travel, entertain, I am also called the boss, the guardian or the chief and many times I have to make the most and the biggest decisions. Who am I?

57) If four women can bake four pies in four hours, how many pies can eight women bake in eight hours?

58) Jeff is younger than Rodney but older than Debbie. Larry is older than Erica who is older than Jeff. Rodney is older than Larry. Who is the middle child?

59) You are all alone in a dark room with a match and matchbox. Nearby you have 3 objects: a candle, an oil lamp and a log of firewood. Which thing do you light first?

60) A hat and scarf cost a total of $1.10. The hat costs $1.00 more than the scarf. How much does the scarf cost?

61) I married your colleagues, I married your friends, I might have even married you, and I married every single girl that asks me to, yet I am still single. Who am I?

62) I can be deep, I can be powerful, I can be complex, blind, difficult, and profound at the same time. What am I?

63) Which word is least like the others? Third, fourth, fifth, sixth, seventh, eighth, ninth?

64) A spider was given $28, an ant was given $21 and a chicken was given $7. How much money did the dog get?

65) If you buy a rooster for the purpose of laying eggs and you hope to have two eggs every day for your breakfast, how many eggs can you expect to have after 13 days?

66) John is taller than Jason. Rebecca is taller than Jason. Sara is taller than John. Beverly is shorter than Rebecca and taller than Sara. Put all people in order of their height.

67) How many crates do you need if you have 304 pairs of shoes and each crate can hold 19 shoes?

68) I come with many colors, so beautiful and bright, I turn so many houses into a beautiful sight. What am I?

69) I am a catchy carol and a tune which likes to rhyme, I contain 12 grand gifts that come around Christmas time. What am I?

70) I am a ball that can be rolled, but never bounced or thrown. What am I?

71) I can be any shape, I can a be surprise to your loved one, just fill me up and make sure to hold me real tight so I won't fly away. What am I?

72) Fill me up with hot or cold, put anything in me I'll make sure I'll hold. What am I?

73) I can be late, I can be early, I can be astronomical or atomic and my insides are incredibly complex. What am I?

74) Sometimes I am bright, sometimes I am dark, I Can be slim, I can Be Fat, some think I am a man but others think I am a rabbit, and I've had a Buzz step on my face. What am I?

75) White and sparkly I can be, fluffy and soft, kids make angels out of me. What am I?

76) I can jump, I can climb, I swing from tree to tree with my many legs and I make a house much bigger than myself. What am I?

77) People look forward to my coming, they light lights for me, they celebrate me, they often take a break and rest when I arrive and some say I am the most important thing all year. What am I?

78) Round and round I go never stopping in a continuous flow. I hang out with numbers each and every day and nothing ever gets in my way. What am I?

79) They provide for you, They love you, they keep you safe, we celebrate them every June. Who are they?

80) I am a stick combined with a sweetness ball. What am I?

81) If you give me a letter I will not keep it long, boxes help pay my salary and I travel so much but never very far. What am I?

82) What five-letter word becomes shorter when you add two letters to it?

83) What has a face and two hands but no arms or legs?

84) What word begins and ends with an *E* but only has one letter?

85) What type of cheese is made backwards?

86) What gets wetter as it dries?

87) What starts with a *P*, ends with an *E* and has thousands of letters?

88) What has to be broken before you can use it?

89) What begins with *T* ends with *T* and has *T* in it?

90) Which month has 28 days?

91) Three men were in a boat. It capsized, but only two got their hair wet. Why?

92) How many letters are there in the alphabet?

93) Tom throws a ball as hard as he can. It comes back to him, even though nothing and nobody touches it. How?

94) Mary's father has five daughters – Nana, Nene, Nini, Nono. What is the fifth daughter's name?

95) What is so delicate that even saying its name breaks it?

96) If an electric train is travelling south, which way is the smoke going?

97) They come out at night without being called, and are lost in the day without being stolen. What are they?

98) What is next in this sequence? JFMAMJJASON...

99) Why do lions eat raw meat?

100) What goes up but never goes down?

Difficult Riddles

101) Why did Mickey Mouse become an astronaut?

102) Why do bees hum?

103) If you threw a White stone into the Red Sea, what would it become?

104) What invention lets you look right through a wall?

105) What has four legs, but can't walk?

106) How do you make the number one disappear?

107) Name three days consecutively where none of the seven days of the week appear.

108) Which word in the dictionary is spelled incorrectly?

109) What is the best cure for dandruff?

110) What did the beach say when the tide came in?

111) Which football player wears the biggest helmet?

112) What did the outlaw get when he stole a calendar?

113) Why did the bumble bee put honey under his pillow?

114) A horse is on a 24 foot chain and wants an apple that is 26 feet away. How can the horse get to the apple?

115) I can sizzle like bacon, I am made with an egg, and I have plenty of backbone, but lack a good leg. I peel layers like onions, but still remain whole; I can be long, like a flagpole, yet fit in a hole. What am I?

116) Who always sleeps with its shoes on?

117) What does a cat have that no other animal can have?

118) Why do dragons sleep all day?

119) What can honk without a horn?

120) It is easy to get into, but hard to get out of? What is it?

121) It has a bark, but no bite. What is it?

122) This can clap without any hands. What is it?

123) It wears a coat, but no pants. What is it?

124) This goes up and down, but never moves? What is it?

125) It flies around all day but never goes anywhere? What is it?

126) This bet can never be won. What is it?

127) This type of dress can never be worn. What is it?

128) You can serve it, but never eat it? What is it?

129) I comfort you so you can have a good night, I am higher without the head, than with it. What am I?

130) Throw away the outside and cook the inside, then eat the outside and throw away the inside. What is it?

131) It stands on one leg with its heart in its head. What is it?

132) You can keep it only after giving it away to someone else. What is it?

133) It has been around for millions of years, It dies and reborn every fifteen days. What is it?

134) It lives without a body, hears without ears, speaks without a mouth, and is born in air. What is it?

135) We see it once in a year, twice in a week, and never in a day. What is it?

136) If I have it, I do not share it. If I share it, I don't have it. What is it?

137) You can hear it, but not touch or see it. What is it?

138) It is round on both sides but high in the middle. What is it?

139)   It gets broken without being held. What is it?

140)   It is always coming but never arrives? What is it?

141)   It has Eighty-eight keys but can't open a single door? What is it?

142)   It has one eye but cannot see? What is it?

143)   It has four eyes but cannot see? What is it?

144)   It has hands but cannot clap? What is it?

145)   It gets beaten, and whipped, but never cries? What is it?

146)   You can catch it, but not throw it? What is it?

147)   This travels around the world but stays in one spot? What is it?

148)   It comes down but never goes up? What is it?

149)   It has a hundred limbs, but cannot walk? What is it?

150)   Take away my first letter, and I still sound the same. Take away my last letter, I still sound the same. Even take away my letter in the middle, I will still sound the same. I am a five letter word. What am I?

151)   I have no bones and no legs, but if you keep me warm, I will soon walk away. What am I?

152)   I am tall when I am young and I am short when I am old. What am I?

153)   When the water comes down, when it rains, I go up over head. What am I?

154) The one who makes me does not need me, when he makes me. The one who buys me does not use me for himself or herself. The one who uses me doesn't know that he or she is using me. What am I?

155) People buy me to eat, but never eat me. What am I?

156) Many times you need me. The more and more you take me further, the more and more you leave me behind. What am I?

157) If you give me water, I will die. What am I?

158) I never ask questions, but always answered. What am I?

159) I have rivers, but do not have water. I have dense forests, but no trees and animals. I have cities, but no people live in those cities. What am I?

160) I have no life, but I can die, what am I?

161) I have no legs. I will never walk, but always run. What am I?

162) I have lots of memories, but I own nothing. What am I?

163) I do not speak, cannot hear or speak anything, but I will always tell the truth. What am I?

164) I do not have wings, but I can fly. I don't have eyes, but I will cry! What am I?

165) I don't have eyes, ears, nose and tongue, but I can see, smell, hear and taste everything. What am I?

166) I am a word. If you pronounce me rightly, it will be wrong. If you pronounce me wrong it is right? What word am I?

167) What kind of room has no doors or windows?

168) What belongs to you but others use it more than you do?

169) I am taken from a mine and shut up in a wooden case, from which I am never released, and yet I am used by almost everybody. What am I?

170) Five men went to church. It started to rain. Four men ran for cover, but got wet on the way. The one man who stayed behind stayed dry. How?

171) What is it that has a bottom at the top of them?

172) What is full of holes, but can still hold a lot of water?

173) What is put on a table and cut, but is never eaten?

174) What kinds of stones are never found in the ocean?

175) As I went across the bridge, I met a man with a load of wood which was neither straight nor crooked. What kind of wood was it?

176) The first man is the master of priceless gems; The second man is the Master of love; The third man is the master of shovels; The fourth Man is the master of big sticks; Who are they?

177) A dad and his son were riding their bikes and crashed. Two ambulances came and took them to different hospitals. The man's son was in the operating room and the doctor said, "I can't operate on you. You're my son." How is that possible?

178) The Smith family is a very wealthy family that lives in a big, circular home. One morning, Mr. Smith woke up and saw a strawberry jam stain on his new

carpet. He figured out that everyone who was there that morning had a jam sandwich. By reading the following excuses, figure out who spilled the jam.

    a. Billy Smith: "I was outside playing basketball."

    b. The Maid: "I was dusting the corners of the house."

    c. Chef: "I was starting to make lunch for later."

       Who is lying?

179) One night, a butcher, a baker, and a candlestick maker go to a hotel. When they get their bill, however, it's for four people. Who's the fourth person?

180) What instrument can you hear but never see?

181) A man was cleaning the windows of a 25 story building. He slipped and fell off the ladder, but wasn't hurt. How did he do it?

182) I have keys but no locks. I have space but no room. You can enter but can't go outside. What am I?

183) Two fathers and two sons go on a fishing trip. They each catch a fish and bring it home. Why do they only bring three home?

184) Tuesday, Sam and Peter went to a restaurant to eat lunch. After eating lunch, they paid the bill. But Sam and Peter did not pay the bill, so who did?

185) What has 4 legs in the morning, 2 legs in the afternoon, and 3 legs at night?

186) If a blue house is made out of blue bricks, a yellow house is made out of yellow bricks and a pink house is made out of pink bricks, what is a greenhouse made of?

187) A house has four walls. All of the walls are facing south, and a bear is circling the house. What color is the bear?

188) What is as light as a feather, but even the world's strongest man couldn't hold it for more than a minute?

189) In a one-story pink house, there was a pink person, a pink cat, a pink fish, a pink computer, a pink chair, a pink table, a pink telephone, a pink shower— everything was pink! What color were the stairs?

190) A man was driving his truck. His lights were not on. The moon was not out. Up ahead, a woman was crossing the street. How did he see her?

191)   What has a head but never weeps, has a bed but never sleeps, can run but never walks, and has a bank but no money?

192)   A man leaves home and turns left three times, only to return home facing two men wearing masks. Who are those two men?

193)   What has many rings, but no fingers?

194)   Can you guess the easiest way to double your money?

195)   Is it possible for any man to go without sleeping for Ten days?

196)   What is as big as an elephant but weighs nothing?

197)   I am a seed with three letters in my name. Take away the last two and I still sound the same. What am I?

198) I get smaller every time I take a bath. What am I?

199) I am black when you buy me, red when you use me and gray when you throw me away. What am I?

200) I go in the water black and come out red. What am I?

Tricky Riddles

201)   I fly without wings. What am I?

202)   Tear me off and scratch my head, what once red is now black. What am I?

203)   I stink while living but smell good when dead. What am I?

204)   If you lose me you may cause people around me to lose me too. What am I?

205)   I am constantly overlooked by everyone but everyone has me. What am I?

206)   I cannot be burned by fire or drowned in water. What am I?

207) I can fall off a building and live, but put me in water I will die. What am I?

208) The faster you run, the harder it is to catch me. What am I??

209) What can point in every direction but can't reach the destination by itself.

210) I reach for the sky, but clutch to the ground; sometimes I leave, but I am always around. What am I?

211) Flat as a leaf, round as a ring; has two eyes, can't see a thing. What is it?

212) I have hundreds of legs but I can only lean; You make me feel dirty so you feel clean. What am I?

213) You can use me to stop; you take me to smoke; Not only do I stop, But I am a stop, And the result of Pool's first stroke. What am I?

214) Where do fish keep their money?

215) What kind of ant is really good at math?

216) If money really did grow on trees, what would be everyone's favorite season?

217) What has one hundred heads and one hundred tails?

218) Why was the basketball player in trouble with the bank?

219) We are sisters from the same mother, but we've never met. Who are the two sisters?

220) What did the boy coffee say to the girl coffee?

221) Why is an island like the letter "T"?

222) What do you call a tick that loves math?

223) Why do you never bring a Pokémon in the bathroom, with you?

224) What ten letter word starts with gas?

225) Why is it so easy to measure fish?

226) Why didn't the skeleton cross the road?

227) I'm am everywhere and a part of everyone. I am at the end of space and time and existence itself. What am I?

228) What has 13 hearts but no other organs?

229) What is 3/7 chicken, 2/3 cat and 2/4 goat?

230) I can't be seen, found, heard or smelled. I lie behind stars and under hills, I fill empty holes, come first and follow after. What am I?

231) What is something that you always have but always leave behind?

232) What room in your house do ghosts avoid?

233) What when read from right to left is a servant but when read from left to right is a ruler?

234) How do you know carrots are good for your eyes?

235) What do you call a fish with 4 eyes?

236) This old one runs forever but never moves at all. He has not lungs nor throat, but still has a mighty roaring call who is he?

237) Why can't you trust the law of gravity?

238) You are my brother but I am not your brother. Who am I?

239) What comes one time in today, three times in tomorrow and never in the future?

240) What can you fill a room with that takes up no space?

241) What city has no people?

242) What does a fish say when it runs into a concrete wall?

243) What has 12 faces and 42 eyes?

244) What time starts and stops with an "n"?

245) Why can't your nose be 12 inches long?

246) Who are people you see every day, but you don't know?

247) Can you write "cow" using thirteen letters?

248) What has one foot and no legs but carries its house?

249) What kind of storm is always in a rush?

250) What is a duck's favorite snack?

251) What's the difference between a well-dressed man on a bicycle and a poorly dressed man on a unicycle?

252) What moves without seeing and cries without eyes?

253) What is the building that you leave without ever having entered?

254) How do you spell hard water with only three letters?

255) I have a large money box, 10 inches wide and 5 inches tall. Roughly how many coins can I place in my empty money box?

256) What does this mean? I RIGHT I

257) You draw a line. Without touching it, how do you make the line longer?

258) How far can a dog run into the woods?

259) If there are three apples and you take away two, how many do you have?

260) How is Europe like a frying pan?

261) You have a five-gallon bucket and a three-gallon bucket with as much water as you need, but no other measuring devices. How do you fill the five-gallon bucket with exactly four gallons of water?

262) Why ghosts are bad liars?

263) How to say Racecar backwards.

264) My name is Ruger. I live on a farm. There are four other dogs on the farm with me. Their names are Snowy, Flash, Speedy, and Brownie. What do you think the fifth dog's name is?

265) I am an odd number. Take away one letter and I become even. What number am I?

266) What word looks the same backwards and upside down?

267) A boy fell off a 20-foot ladder but did not get hurt. Why not?

268) Using only addition, how do you add eight 8s and get the number 1,000?

269) Dead on the field lie ten soldiers in white, felled by three eyes, black as night. What happened?

270) Turn us on our backs and open up our stomachs you will be the wisest of men though at start a lummox.

271) What word in the English language uses all five vowels plus Y in alphabetical order, and uses each only once?

272) What is the only English word, with two synonyms that are antonyms of each other?

273) I am the outstretched fingers that seize and hold the wind. Wisdom flows from me in other hands. Upon me are sweet dreams dreamt. My merest touch brings laughter. What am I?

274) It's always in front of you but cannot be seen?

275) I drive men mad for love of me, easily beaten, never free.

Genius Riddles

276) A house of wood in a hidden place. Built without nails or glue. High above the earthen ground It holds pale gems of blue.

277) Through wind and rain I always play, I roam the earth, yet here I stay; I crumble stones, and fire cannot burn me; yet I am soft- you can shear me with your hand.

278) What building has the most stories?

279) What has four fingers and one thumb, but isn't alive?

280) What can never be put in a saucepan?

281) Two fathers and two sons are in a car, yet there are only three people in the car. How is this possible?

282) What brute strength struggles to get through, I make it easy for you to undo. What am I?

283) After a fall, you'll always find me there. What once was alive, will now be bare. What am I?

284) An instrument through which sounds are made, and yet, not something that can be played. What am I?

285) You are lost in the woods and the path you are following forks into two: a path to the left and one to the right. One path will lead you to safety while the other will cause you to be lost forever. At the fork are two twin sisters who know which path is which. The sisters are identical in every way except one: one of the sisters always tells the truth while the other always lies. You can ask only one question and you don't know which sister is which. What can you ask them so you know which path to take?

286) There are three chests, each of which contains 100 coins. One chest has 100 gold coins, one has 100 silver coins, and the third has an equal split of 50 gold coins and 50 silver coins. Each chest is labeled, but all are labeled incorrectly. You are allowed to pick one coin from just one of the chests and after his you must correctly identify each of the three chests. What should you do?

287) Turn me on my side and I am everything. Cut me in half and I am nothing. What am I?

288) You have two ropes, each of which takes exactly one hour to burn if lit from one end. The ropes are not identical, nor are they uniform, i.e. it doesn't necessarily take half an hour for half the rope to burn. With only these two ropes and a way to light them, how do you measure out 45 minutes?

289) You want to boil an egg for exactly 15 minutes but you only own a 7-minute hourglass and an 11-minute hourglass. How can you achieve what you want?

290) What jumps when it walks and sits when it stands?

291) If you eat me, my sender will eat you, What am I?

292) A man is found murdered in his office. The suspects are Peter, Julie, Jason, Molly and Brian. In the office is a calendar with the numbers 6,4,9,10,11 written in blood. Who is the killer?

293) Our dinner guests cry that we are evil, when they notice their place in the meal. But its no big deal why; we are just one big happy tribe! And we get real fed up with people! Who, What or Are we?

294) Lighter than what I am made of, More of me is hidden than is seen. What am I?

295) Two women apply for a job. They are identical and have the same mother, father and birthday. The interviewer asks, "Are you twins?" to which they honestly reply, "No".
How is this possible?

296) I am a vegetable that bugs stay away from. What am I?

297) What is it that has a power socket on one end and a corkscrew on the other?

298) A man walks out of a house that has four walls all facing north. A bird walks past him. What is it?

299) Where is there is no south, west, nor east, and weather not fit for man or beast, what is it?

300) What animal would you get crossed a duck, a beaver, and an otter?

301) It lives in winter, dies in summer, and grows with its roots on top? What is it?

302) What's green, but not a leaf; copies others, but is not a monkey?

303) I use my ear to speak and my mouth to hear. What am I?

304) It's a shower in name of newborn baby but without water. What is it?

305) What has teeth, but cannot chew?

306) I can carry lots of food, I keep it cool, but cannot eat anything.

307) It can see, but it isn't an eye, A carpenter made me, and not God. What am I?

308) You can eat me at night, but never in the morning. What am I?

309) I am hard like white-stone, but I grow on your body. I fall apart but I come back stronger, Guess who Am I?

310) I'm excellent to taste, but horrible to smell. What am I?

311) I have lots of money, but I need someone else to carry me around to spend it. What am I?

312) I'm a single digit number having no value. Which digit am I?

313) How many animals did Moses take on the ark?

314) What is something you can put in your pocket that keeps it empty?

315) A man started route to town with a fox, a goose, and a sack of corn. He came to a stream which he had to cross in a tiny boat. He could only take one across at a time. He could not leave the fox alone with the goose or the goose alone with the corn. How did he get them all safely over the stream?

316) There were two ducks in front of a duck, two ducks behind a duck, and one duck in the middle. How many ducks were there in total?

317) What type of vehicle is spelled the same backwards and forwards?

318) What did one falling leaf say to another?

319)	Why are all Superman costumes tight?

320)	Why do birds fly south in the fall?

321)	What do you use to mend a jack-o-lantern?

322)	What did scientists say when they found 2 isotopes of Helium?

323)	What is the "center" of gravity?

324)	If dogs have fleas, what do sheep have?

325)	Why do you see frogs look so happy?

326)	What house can fly?

327)	A man in tights is knocked out by a rock next to him. The rock did not touch him. What happened to him?

328) I'm fat and I'm round and I cause much joy, I'm often end up being a dog's favorite toy. What am I?

329) There are 50 crows on a wire, a hunter shoots and kills three. How many are there left on the wire?

330) John has 22 apples in a basket. Meghan and Dave both take 2 and you take 16 how many apples do you have?

331) What is the best way to keep your hat from falling off your head?

332) What has 6 wheels and flies?

333) What brings you down but never up?

334) To dye a single Easter egg takes 7.5 minutes if you leave it in dye. How long would it take to dye 3 eggs?

335) A man walks all the way around the world without getting up. How does he do this?

336) What do thief's get for stealing calendars?

337) You   struggle   to   regain   me. When   I'm   lost,   you   struggle   to   obtain   me. I   pass   no   matter   your   will, but   I'm   your   slave   to   kill. What am I?

338) I have four wings, but cannot fly. I never laugh and never cry; on the same spot I'm always found, toiling away with a little sound. What am I?

339) A man and his boss have the same parents, but are not siblings. How is this possible?

340) I am a cave full of bones, and the house of a worm. What am I?

341) Soft and cuddly, I'll pull on your heart. But take my last name and I'll tear you apart. What am I?

342) This is an unusual paragraph. I'm curious as to just how quickly you can find out what is so unusual about it. It looks so ordinary and plain that you would think nothing was wrong with it. In fact, nothing is wrong with it! It is highly unusual though. Study it and think about it, but you still may not find anything odd. But if you work at it a bit, you might find out. Try to do so without any coaching!

343) You walk into a room with a rabbit holding a carrot, a pig eating slop, and a chimp holding a banana. Which animal in the room is the smartest?

344) There are three jars full of equal number of quarters, dimes, and penny's in each of them. Which one has the highest value?

345) I make disappear the darkness but live in the shade. What am I?

346) If you count 20 houses on your right going to the store and 20 houses on your left coming back home, how many different houses did you count?

347) Three men rob a store but come out completely changed. Yet they continue robbing other stores. What kind of store did they first rob?

348) A pet shop owner had a parrot with a sign on its cage that said "Parrot repeats everything it hears." A young man bought the parrot and for two weeks he spoke to it but it didn't say a word. He tried to return

the parrot but the shopkeeper said he never lied. How can this be?

349) How do you share 34 apples among 33 people?

350) A boy at a carnival went to a booth ran by a man who said "If I can write your exact weight on this piece of paper then you have to give me $50, but if I cannot, I will pay you $50." The boy looked around and saw no scale so he agreed, thinking no matter what the carny writes he'll just say he weighs more or less. In the end the boy ended up paying the man $50. How did the man win the bet?

351) Can you rearrange the letters in new door to make one word?

352) At the sound of me, men may dream or stamp their feet. At the sound of me, women may laugh or sometimes weep. Who am I?

353) For me, I slap you. Because of you, I slap me. Hitting your skin, My blood flows. Who Am I?

354) I dig out tiny caves, and store gold and silver in them. I also build bridges of silver and make crowns of gold. They are the smallest you could imagine. Sooner or later everybody needs my help, yet many people are afraid to let me help them. Who am I?

355) I have all the knowledge you have. But I am small as your fist that your hands can hold me. Who am I?

356) I'm sometimes a soldier; That's part of an army; I'm also an insect That lives in a castle made of soil.

357) I was a famous pirate, One who was truly feared Had a dark color and some facial hair. My name is _ _ _ _ _.

358) In March or April These things do abound; Sometimes these are hollow And have chocolate inside A certain bunny leaves these on the ground. What Am I?

359) I'm sometimes dark but I'm not a room with curtains; I sometimes contain peanut butter but I'm not a sandwich; I'm can be sometimes melted but I'm not an ice cube; I'm sometimes in cookies but I'm not a raisin; I'm sometimes a bar but I'm not made of metal; I'm sometimes a chip but I'm not made of potato. What Am I?

360) I have stripes but I'm not a zebra; I look like a hook but have nothing to do with Peter Pan; I'm normally red and white but I'm not the Canadian flag; I can be eaten but I'm not a strawberry jelly sandwich; I'm usually seen at Christmas But I'm not a stocking or a bell. Can you guess what am I?

361) If you see this hairy creature; you'll be crippled in fear; It appears only on a full moon. Still you're not running because you've got silver bullets in a gun. Can you name this creature?

362) If you're sailing on a pirate ship
To find your way you'll need at least
This item that will help guide the way
By pointing its finger to keep going the sail. Can you tell what am I?

363) I'm a strongest stone,
A red card But I am not a heart;
Of an engagement ring, I am usually most beautiful part who steals women's heart; Tell me please if you know my name!

364) A legendary creature; whose fiery breath can be quite ruthless; in movies about how to train them;

The main one went by the name Toothless! Do you know who am I?

365) We are known for having pointy ears and for making Christmas toys which are delivered by Santa to All of the good girls and boys! Do you know who we are?

Answers

Clever Riddle Answers

1) A donkey and a monkey.

2) A keyboard.

3) A rainbow.

4) An airplane.

5) 16 bicycles.

6) A jersey.

7) Kiwi.

8) The eldest son because it was December in New York and the lawn wouldn't need mowing.

9) Exactly at TWOoth o'clock.

10) A bloodhound.

11) Later.

12) It can't do any of the above because the fly is already dead.

13) They all have spots.

14) A balloon.

15) Ostrich, because all the other birds can fly.

16) Nicole and Brad were married and are therefore not single.

17) The letter R.

18) Polar bears because their fur is actually colorless.

19) Money.

20) Because rabbits don't have hair, they have fur.

21) A tomato.

22) They both weigh exactly the same, one ton.

23) In the dictionary.

24) They both have fans.

25) Apples.

26) Breakfast.

27) The letter A.

28) Zero, because rubber ducks aren't alive and cannot drown.

29) A cartoon.

30) Water.

31) The letter S.

32) Shoes.

33) A shadow.

34) A toilet.

35) Stop imagining.

36) The Word "Hilarious".

37) Three. Each circle within a number is equivalent to one. For example, the numbers 9 and 6 are equivalent to one because they have one circle in them, whereas the number 8 is equal to 2 because of its two loops.

38) A knife.

39) A house full of gadgets.

40) Rice.

41) 7000 (k is a symbol for 1000 USD).

42) A coin.

43) I am poop.

44) Add me.

45) A bank.

46) Glasses.

47) The Netherlands.

48) They all have a new version. (New Mexico, New Jersey, New Castle, New Delhi...etc.)

49) Donald Duck.

50) I have way too many problems.

51) The letter U.

52) Just one: January 2nd

53) In Pole-Land.

54) You seem surprised to see me.

55) Emoji's.

56) The president.

57) 16 pies.

58) Erica.

59) The match.

60) $0.05 (not $0.10).

61) A priest.

62) Love.

63) Third, it is the only one not ending in "th".

64) $14 ($3.50 per leg).

65) Zero, roosters don't lay eggs.

66) Rebecca, Beverly, Sara, John and Jason.

67) 32 crates (608 shoes ÷ 19 = 32).

68) Christmas lights.

69) The 12 days of Christmas song.

70) Eyeball.

71) A Balloon.

72) A cup.

73) Clock.

74) The moon.

75) Snow.

76) Spider.

77) Christmas.

78) The hands of a clock.

79) Dads.

80) Lollipop.

81) A postman.

82) Short.

83) A clock.

84) Envelope.

85) Edam.

86) A towel.

87) Post-Office.

88) An egg.

89) A teapot.

90) All of them, of course.

91) One was bald.

92) Eleven – T-h-e A-l-p-h-a-b-e-t.

93) He throws it straight up.

94) If you answered Nunu, you are wrong. It is Mary!

95) Silence.

96) There is no smoke; it is an electric train!

97) Stars.

98) The letter "D." The sequence contains the first letter of each month.

99) Because they never learned to cook.

100) Your age.

Difficult Riddle Answers

101) He wanted to visit Pluto.

102) Because they do not know the words.

103) Wet.

104) A window.

105) A table.

106) Add the letter G and it's "gone".

107) Yesterday, Today, and Tomorrow.

108) Incorrectly.

109) Baldness.

110) Long time, no sea.

111) The one with the biggest head.

112) Twelve months.

113) He wanted to have sweet dreams.

114) By walking to Apple, the chain is not attached to anything.

115) A snake.

116) A horse.

117) Kittens.

118) They like to hunt knights.

119) A goose.

120) Trouble.

121) A tree.

122) Thunder.

123) A Book.

124) A flight of stairs.

125) A Flag.

126) The alphabet.

127) An address.

128) A tennis ball.

129) A pillow.

130) Corn on the cob – because you throw away the husk, cook and eat the kernels, and throw away the cob.

131) A cabbage.

132) Your word of promise.

133) The moon.

134) An echo.

135) The letter "E".

136) A secret.

137) Your voice.

138) Ohio.

139) A promise.

140) Tomorrow.

141) A piano.

142) A needle.

143) Mississippi (word has four 'i's).

144) A clock.

145) An egg.

146) A cold.

147) A Post stamp.

148) Rain.

149) A tree.

150) Empty.

151) An egg.

152) A candle.

153) An umbrella.

154) A coffin.

155) A plate.

156) Footsteps.

157) Fire.

158) A doorbell.

159) A map.

160) A battery.

161) A river.

162) A photo album.

163) A mirror.

164) A cloud.

165) A brain.

166) Wrong.

167) A mushroom.

168) Your name.

169) Pencil lead.

170) The dry man was a body in a coffin and the other four were pall bearers.

171) Your legs.

172) A Sponge.

173) A pack of cards.

174) Stones that are dry.

175) Sawdust.

176) The kings in a deck of cards.

177) The doctor is his mom!

178) It was the maid. The house is circular; it has no corners.

179) One night can also mean one knight. That makes four: one knight, a butcher, a baker and a candlestick maker!

180) Your voice! You can sing with your voice like an instrument and hear it, but no one can see it!

181) He fell off the second step.

182) A keyboard

183) The fishing trip consists of a grandfather, a father and a son.

184) Their friend, Tuesday.

185) A person! As a baby you crawl (4 legs), as an adult you walk (2 legs), then when you are older you use a cane (3 legs).

186) Glass.

187) The house is on the North Pole, so the bear is white.

188) His breath.

189) There were not any stairs; it was a one-story house!

190) It was a bright and sunny day.

191) A river.

192) A catcher and an umpire (Baseball Game).

193) A telephone.

194) Put it in front of the mirror.

195) It is possible as we all sleep through the night and not during the day.

196) The shadow of an elephant.

197) A pea.

198) A bar of soap.

199) Charcoal.

200) Lobster.

<u>Tricky Riddles Answers</u>

201) Time.

202) A matchstick.

203) Grilled Pig. (Bacon)

204) Your temper.

205) A nose.

206) Ice.

207) Paper.

208) Your breath.

209) Your finger.

210) I am Tree.

211) A button.

212) A Broom.

213) Brake/ Break.

214) Riverbanks.

215) An accountant.

216) Fall.

217) One hundred pennies.

218) He kept bouncing checks.

219) Day and night.

220) I love you a latte.

221) Because both are in the middle of the water. (T is the middle word of "water")

222) A arithmetic.

223) They might pickatchu! (peek at you)

224) Automobile.

225) Because they come with their own scales.

226) He did not have the guts.

227) The letter E.

228) Deck Of Cards.

229) Chicago.

230) The dark.

231) Fingerprints.

232) The living room.

233) God.

234) You never see rabbits wearing glasses.

235) Fiiiish.

236) A waterfall.

237) Because it will always let you down.

238) Your sister.

239) The letter 'O'.

240) Light.

241) Electricity.

242) Dam.

243) A pair of dice.

244) Noon.

245) Because it would be a foot!

246) Strangers.

247) See o double you.

248) A snail.

249) Hurricane.

250) Quackers.

251) A tire.

252) A cloud.

253) The hospital that you were born in.

254) ICE.

255) Just one, after which it will no longer be empty.

256) Right between the eyes.

257) You draw a shorter line next to it, and it becomes the longer line.

258) The dog can run into the woods only halfway – if it ran any farther it would run out of the woods!

259) If you take two apples, then of course you have two.

260) Because it has Greece at the bottom.

261) Fill the five-gallon bucket all the way up. Pour it into the three-gallon bucket until it is full. Empty the three-gallon bucket. Pour the remaining two gallons into the three-gallon bucket. Fill the five-gallon bucket all the way up, then finish filling the three-gallon bucket, leaving four gallons in the five-gallon bucket.

262) Because you can see right through them.

263) "Racecar backwards."

264) Ruger.

265) Seven. (take away the "s" and it becomes "even")

266) SWIMS.

267) He fell off the bottom step.

268) 888 + 88 + 8 + 8 + 8 = 1000.

269) A bowling ball knocked down ten pins.

270) Book.

271) Facetiously.

272) Cleave.

273) Feather.

274) Future.

275) Gold.

Genius Riddle Anwers

276) Nest.

277) Ocean.

278) The library.

279) A glove.

280) Its lid.

281) They are grandfather, father and son.

282) A key.

283) Winter.

284) Your voice.

285) Ask one of the sisters which path their sister would tell you to take.

Let's say the left hand path is the correct one to follow.

The sister that lies knows their truthful sister would tell you the left hand path, so as they always lie they will tell you the right hand path.

The honest sister knows their lying sister will tell you the right hand path and because they're honest, they will tell you this. So you should follow the opposite path to that which you are told, regardless of which sister tells you.

286) Take a coin from the chest labeled 50/50.

If you pick a gold coin, you know that chest must contain all gold coins (it can't be the 50/50 chest because all the chests are incorrectly labeled). So the chest labelled silver must be the 50/50 chest and the one labeled gold must be the silver chest.

On the other hand if you pick a silver coin, you know that chest must contain all silver coins, the one labeled silver must be the gold chest and the one labeled gold must be the 50/50 chest.

287) The number 8. On its side, it looks like the symbol for infinity and when you cut it in half, it looks like two zeroes.

288) You can do this in the following way:

First, light both ends of one rope and only one end of the other rope. This will cause the first rope to burn out in 30 minutes (as you lit both ends it will burn in half the time as if you'd only lit one end). When the first rope burns out, there will be 30 minutes left on the second rope (as each rope takes one hour to burn when lit from one end).

So then, light the other end of the second rope so both ends of it are now burning. This rope will now burn out in another 15 minutes.

The total time elapsed at this point will be 45 minutes   (30 + 15 = 45 minutes).

289) Turn both hourglasses over as you start boiling the egg.

After 7 minutes the 7-minute hourglass will run out. Turn it over to start again.

In another 4 minutes the 11-minute hourglass will run out.

At this point, turn over the 7-minute hourglass. It will now take another 4 minutes to run out.

When it does so, your egg will have been boiling for exactly 15 minutes (7 minutes + 4 minutes + 4 minutes).

290) A kangaroo.

291) A fish hook.

292) Jason is the killer.

The numbers indicate months and the first letter of each month spells the name of the murderer, e.g. the 6th month is June and the first letter of June is J, the 4th month is April and the first letter of April is a, and so on.

293) Cannibals!

294) An iceberg.

295) They are triplets.

296) Squash.

297) A Pig. (Nose And Tail)

298) Penguin.

299) The South Pole.

300) A platypus.

301) An icicle.

302) A parrot.

303) A Phone.

304) A baby shower.

305) A comb.

306) A refrigerator.

307) A keyhole.

308) Dinner! Dinner can never be had in the morning because it's dinner!

309) A tooth.

310) A tongue.

311) A wallet/purse. It holds all our money, but does it spend it?

312) Zero.

313) Moses didn't take anything on the ark. Noah did.

314) A large hole.

315) He took the goose over first and came back. Then he took the fox across and brought the goose back. Next, he took the corn over. He came back alone and took the goose.

316) Three ducks standing in line.

317) Racecar!

318) I'm falling for you.

319) They're all size S.

320) Because it's too far to walk.

321) A pumpkin patch.

322) They said "HeHe"

323) The letter "v": gra-v-ity.

324) Sheep have fleece.

325) Because they eat buggers that bugs them.

326) Housefly.

327) The rock is kryptonite and the man is Superman.

328) A ball.

329) None, the sound made them fly away.

330) 16.

331) Don't put it on your head.

332) A garbage truck!

333) Gravity.

334) 7.5 minutes. Do them all at once.

335) He is imagining it in his head.

336) 12 months.

337) Time.

338) A Ceiling fan.

339) He is self-employed. He is his own boss.

340) Your mouth. The inside of a mouth is full of teeth and looks like a cave. The worm is your tongue.

341) A teddy bear.

342) The letter E, which is the most common letter used in the English language, does not appear in the paragraph.

343) You are the smartest animal in the room (hopefully).

344) The jar full of quarters would have the highest value because a quarter is worth more than a dime and penny.

345) A lamp.

346) 20, they are the same houses.

347) A luxury clothing store. They changed clothes.

348) The parrot was deaf!

349) Make Applesauce.

350) The man did exactly as he said he would and wrote "your exact weight" on the paper.

351) Yes, it's an anagram. 'New door' and 'one word' contain the same letters.

352) Music.

353) Mosquito.

354) The Dentist.

355) I'm your brain!

356) Ant.

357) Blackbeard.

358) Easter Eggs.

359) Chocolate.

360) Candy Cane.

361) A Werewolf.

362) A Compass.

363) Diamond.

364) A Dragon.

365) We are Elf's!

Thank You Note

Thank you for making it through to the end of this **massive collection of Riddles For Genius Kids.** Let's hope this book was informative and helped everybody who read and had fun time with their friends and families.

Riddles are a centuries-old tradition and some riddles have been found actually recorded in ancient civilizations. They teach us critical thinking as well as further developing the ability to look for answers outside of the normal way of thinking.

So have some friends over and challenge each other to a riddle duel. Get your family together for some quality time and teach your children the value of using and strengthening their minds. This book has given you the opportunity to have some of the best and most thought-provoking riddles in one place, making it easy to have fun with them every now and then.

Finally, if you found this book useful in any way, A **Review on Amazon** is always appreciated! We Look Forward For Any Suggestions.

Thank You Again...
-Mike.

34317031R10121

Made in the USA
Middletown, DE
25 January 2019